JESUS
IS YOUR
HEALER

THE POWER OF HIS SACRIFICE
BOTH TO SAVE AND TO HEAL

DENISE RENNER

Jesus Is Your Healer —
The Power of His Sacrifice Both To Save and To Heal
ISBN: 978-1-6675-0448-3
eBook: 987-1-6675-0449-0
Copyright © 2024 by Denise Renner
1814 W. Tacoma St.
Broken Arrow, OK 74012

Published by Harrison House
Shippensburg, PA 17257-2914
www.harrisonhouse.com

2 3 4 5 6 / 28 27 26 25 24

Editorial Consultants: Cynthia D. Hansen and Rebecca L. Gilbert
Text Design: Lisa Simpson, www.SimpsonProductions.net
Cover Design: Lisa M. Moore

CONTENTS

Part 2
HEAVEN'S KEYS TO UNLOCK YOUR HEALING

FOREWORD

by Rick Renner

This is *hands down* the best book
I've ever read on the subject of healing!

You might say, "Well, Rick, of course you're going to say that, because it is written by your wife." But the truth really is that I was quite stunned as I read this book. Over the years of my ministry, I have read many books on healing, and I absolutely did not expect that this one would be the best I have ever read on the subject. When I've read books by Denise in the past, I've offered suggestions for her — but this time, I couldn't think of a thing to add or change. I was completely *wowed* by it.

Denise has a powerful testimony about the healing power of Jesus Christ in her own life, and that is why she writes with such authority, compassion, and power on this important subject that touches all of us. The subtitle of this book says the sacrifice of Jesus was designed both to save us and to heal us. And in this book, Denise makes it clear that His sacrificial death and every drop of His shed blood happened to purchase our salvation *and* our healing of every kind. Indeed, Jesus is our Savior, but He is also our *Healer.* He is in the business not only of saving us for all eternity, but also of healing us and giving our lives back to us.

In fact, Denise makes this so clear that it caused me to wonder why the wonderful church I attended when I was growing up never embraced the healing power of Jesus. I had never heard that

Jesus also shed His blood to pay the price for my healing, and I had never seen anyone healed in my growing-up days — *not ever*.

I know there are many people who are like me — who are saved, but they have never heard that Jesus' blood was shed to heal them as well as to save them. All they know about Jesus' power is what they have read in the Bible. Never having personally witnessed His miracle-working power, they can only fantasize and try to imagine what His miracles must have been like. That means what they know about Jesus' healing and miracle-working power is purely mental or imaginary — it's similar to how they might view the hero in a fairy tale or legend.

But God never intended for Jesus the Healer to be just a historical figure who did something miraculous in the past. That is why Denise writes, "The Holy Spirit doesn't want you to just say, 'Oh, yes, Jesus is the Miracle Worker in Matthew, Mark, Luke, and John.' No, He wants you to *know* beyond a shadow of a doubt: 'Jesus is *my* Miracle Worker!'"

Denise jubilantly adds, "Today I can't help but preach about the power in the stripes of Jesus both to heal and deliver us, because I've been healed again and again and have received miracles in my own life."

As you will see in the pages of this book, sickness is a thief — but Jesus is a Restorer. He has conquered sickness and disease on the Cross with His own blood, and He made sure we can experience healing power. As Denise says, "If you have sickness, pain, or disease — anything that's trying to attach itself to your body — the will of God absolutely is to heal you. *Can* He heal you? Yes, He is the God of the impossible! He most assuredly *can* heal you. And He is the same yesterday, today, and forever, so you can also know beyond a shadow of a doubt that today, He *wants* to heal you...."

Jesus paid too great a price to free us from sickness for us to give up standing in faith for our healing. And if we haven't seen the manifestation of what we're believing for, Denise exhorts, "Just keep your eyes on the Healer. As you draw near to Jesus, you move toward your miracle. Listen to His voice above all others, for in His voice is deliverance. As your heart agrees with His promises and your mouth speaks what He has said, *your* voice becomes the delivering voice of God in your situation, and your faith will make you whole."

I am confident that as you read this book, you will be encouraged not to give up — that if you will agree with the Word of God and the Greater One inside you, you *will* push through to your miracle!

If you (or someone you know) are struggling with symptoms, including pain, or you're feeling oppressed in your mind and emotions — I encourage you that this book is filled with what you need to cause your faith to reach out and grab hold of the healing that Jesus purchased for you. In fact, the goal of this book is to enable every reader to personally proclaim: "Jesus *is* my Healer! God is faithful and His promises are true!"

Denise makes one statement that's so powerful, it should be quoted by other preachers, teachers, and believers worldwide: "EVERY DROP OF JESUS' BLOOD HAD OUR NAME ON IT!" Friend, there is a miracle of healing waiting for you that was paid for by Jesus' precious blood!

It is my greatest honor to write this foreword and I plan to do all I can to get this book into as many hands as possible, for I know it will result in many receiving the healing touch that Jesus purchased for them on the Cross! I am sure this book was divinely placed in your hands and that it will unlock the healing that Jesus' shed blood purchased for you.

Don't stop with Jesus only being your Savior, for He also died to be your *Healer*!

Rick Renner
Minister, Author, Broadcaster
Moscow, Russia

PREFACE

One day as I was reading John 18, I was meditating on all the events that took place and all the words spoken between Jesus and Pilate during the hours when Jesus was being prepared for crucifixion. Then I read John 19:1, where it says, "...Pilate took Jesus and scourged Him."

Pilate took Jesus and scourged Him.

I started thinking about the horror of all Jesus went through that is encompassed in those six simple words. I thought of His cruel beating — the whips tipped with metal and glass that wrapped around Jesus' body and cut into His flesh, each violent swing empowered by the masses' angry screams and the vengeance of the Roman soldier. I thought of Jesus' blood splattering onto the ground and covering every inch of His body, from His face down to His feet, as the soldier continued to lay blow after blow across His battered body. Yet Jesus endured it all as the spotless Lamb of God led to the slaughter (*see* Isaiah 53:7).

As I meditated on the horrific details of Jesus' scourging, all described in six simple words, I thought to myself, *Those wounds Jesus received from that cruel whipping are still providing healing for cancer; still providing healing for diseases of the eyes, lungs, and skin; still providing healing for diabetes. Because of the stripes He endured, there is healing for children who are born with deformities. There is healing for blindness. Within those six short words in John 19:1, there is healing for every disease, infirmity, and pain known to man!*

That's why I wrote this book — so that through the power of the Holy Spirit, God can use the words contained in these pages to paint this eternal truth on the canvas of your mind and heart: *Jesus is your Healer.* When that happens and you claim that spiritual reality as your very own, you will receive all the magnificent power that is extended *to* you through the horrible beating Jesus endured *for* you.

I pray that you take the time to meditate on the powerful truths contained in this book, and I urge you to revisit this message again and again to refresh and strengthen your faith in your covenant right to walk in divine health. As you do, God will deeply imprint on your heart once and for all that Jesus is your Healer and that more than 2,000 years ago, He paid the full price — all that would ever be necessary — to heal *you.*

Denise Renner
Moscow, Russia

INTRODUCTION

We're living in what the Bible calls the last days — the period of time in God's plan that began on the Day of Pentecost and continues to this hour. But as my husband Rick teaches, Scripture reveals that this present-day generation is living in *the very last* of the last days. We can tell by all the events taking place in our world today that it is no longer "life as usual." We're drawing close to that time when Jesus will return for His Church!

With all that's happening in this hour, it's so important that we are strong in our spiritual foundation. One vital part of that foundation must be our absolute knowledge that *Jesus is our Healer*. Once this is truly revelation knowledge to us, we'll hold a vital key to help us stay strong and effective in the building of our spiritual house.

We live in a fallen world, and at times sickness tries to come on us or our loved ones. We are also living in *the last of the last days*, with a plethora of diseases all around us. We're continually hearing of new outbreaks, new variants of viruses, and another person coming down with this or that. The pressure of the days we're living in is increasing.

Yet in the midst of it all, we never have to bow to sickness, because we have the Healer! Although a thousand may fall at our side and ten thousand at our right hand, we can become "germ graveyards" (as I've heard our friend Andrew Wommack say)! We can fill our heart with faith that the sicknesses and plagues of this world will *not* come near our dwelling because of Jesus' power to save, deliver, and heal (*see* Psalm 91:3-10)!

We don't get to that place of faith overnight. It comes from our meditating on and confessing God's promises as a lifestyle. It's a decision we must make every single day: "No, I'm *not* going the way of the world. I have the resurrection power of Jesus on the inside of me!"

Friend, we don't want our mind just filled with all the facts about Jesus' divine power to heal, yet we aren't experiencing Him as our personal Healer. Jesus *is* the Healer. He is *my* Healer. He is *your* Healer.

When Jesus was on the earth, He would preach; He would teach; and He would demonstrate the power of God. Jesus healed and delivered so many people and performed so many miracles. But Jesus doesn't want us to know that He is a Miracle Worker just with our mind — because we read about Him performing miracles in Matthew, Mark, Luke, and John. He is not interested only in our mental assent about who He is. He wants His mighty power to heal and make whole to become a *living reality* in our lives!

Jesus wants us to have an expectation in our heart that the healing He has already purchased for us is going to manifest as physical wholeness for ourselves and our families. He wants us to *experience* Him as *our* Miracle Worker!

We know that Jesus is the same yesterday, today, and forever (*see* Hebrews 13:8). Just as He was a Miracle Worker 2,000 years ago, He is a Miracle Worker today — and He wants you to receive *your* miracle.

I'm believing that even as you read this book, your eyes will be opened to this truth in a more tangible way that brings wholeness to your body and great stability to what you believe and experience. Every truth contained in these pages leads to one conclusion: Jesus *wants* to see you *healed, whole,* and *strong* in your spirit, soul, and body and in every area of your life. He wants you to be well able to navigate these "last of the last days," living triumphantly over every form of sickness and disease!

Jesus is the same yesterday, today, and forever. Just as He was a Miracle Worker 2,000 years ago, He is a Miracle Worker today — and He wants you to receive *your* miracle.

PART 1

HEALING IS YOURS!

1

~

IS IT GOD'S WILL
TO HEAL *YOU*?

Have you ever wondered why some people are healed and some are not? You probably have asked that question at one time or another. But could one answer be that some who seek so hard for their healing really don't know, or are not convinced, of the amazing, overpowering love of God that is the basis for His desire to heal?

I want to show you in Scripture that God *wants* you to come before Him with confidence.

Now this is the confidence that we have in Him, that if we ask anything according to His will, He hears us. And if we know that He hears us, whatever we ask, we know that we have the petitions that we have asked of Him.

1 John 5:14,15

If you're a parent, just think of how you want your own children to approach you if they need something. You don't want your child coming before you with his head hanging down, begging you. You don't want your child saying to you, "I know I'm not worthy, and I don't know whether or not you really love me or whether you actually want to bless me or help me. But here I go, Dad (or Mom) — I'm going to give it a try and ask you for what I want."

No, you want your child to feel free to come to you and say, "You know, Dad, I'd really like to have a bicycle!"

What child have you ever seen who doesn't know what to write down on his or her Christmas wish list? What child says, "Well, I really don't know what I want this Christmas"? No, most children absolutely know what they want! And most also know without question that their parents want to be a blessing to them.

Well, how much more does the Heavenly Father want to be a blessing to you and me? Of course, He does. His Son Jesus gave up everything to come to the earth to save and deliver us and give us peace of mind. The Father absolutely wants to give us good things (*see* Romans 8:32).

> **"If you then, being evil, know how to give good gifts to your children, how much more will *your* heavenly Father give the Holy Spirit to those who ask Him!"**
>
> **Luke 11:13**

> **"Do not fear, little flock, for it is your Father's good pleasure to give you the kingdom."**
>
> **Luke 12:32**

So we can see in the Scriptures that knowing God's will is very important. And we know He hasn't changed. We know that whatever His will was in the past, it is still His will today because the Bible says He is the same yesterday, today, and forever and that

He doesn't change (*see* Hebrews 13:8). You and I may change, but God *never* changes.

The Bible also says that Jesus is the express image of the Father.

God, who at various times and in various ways spoke in time past to the fathers by the prophets, has in these last days spoken to us by His Son, whom He has appointed heir of all things, through whom also He made the worlds; who being the brightness of His glory and the express image of His person....

Hebrews 1:1-3

When we look at Jesus, we see the Father. In fact, we often say, especially at Christmastime, that Jesus is the incarnation of God. He is God who "...became flesh and dwelt among us..." (*see* John 1:14). So what do we see Jesus doing throughout His earthly ministry as He dwelled "among us"? For one thing, we see Him *healing people*.

The Holy Spirit wants to give you confidence through the Scriptures that you can come boldly before the Lord and believe Him for your healing. Jesus healed people then, and He heals people today. Jesus lived on this earth as the express image and will of the Father — so you can know beyond a shadow of a doubt that it is the Father's will to heal *you*.

Jesus healed people then, and He heals people today. Jesus lived on this earth as the express image and will of the Father — so you can know beyond a shadow of a doubt that it is the Father's will to heal *you*.

In Luke 4:18, we see a description of what Jesus wanted to do when He came. Jesus was reading in the synagogue from what we know as the book of Isaiah — and He was prophesying about Himself as He read out loud and declared this.

> **"The Spirit of the Lord is upon Me, because He has anointed Me to preach the gospel to the poor; He has sent Me to heal the brokenhearted, to proclaim liberty to the captives and recovery of sight to the blind, to set at liberty those who are oppressed."**
>
> **Luke 4:18**

- If you're brokenhearted today, it is God's will to heal your heart.

- If you're bound by some kind of addiction or bondage, it's His will to deliver you from whatever holds you captive.

- If you are emotionally bruised — if you have been put down or have suffered under the hand of another — it is God's will to set you free.

- If you have problems with your eyes, it is His will to heal your eyes.

- It is God's will to heal *any* part of you!

So we see that this is not only the will of the Father, but this is also Jesus' will, because Jesus is the express image of the Father.

HIS COMPASSIONS ARE NEW EVERY MORNING

Lamentations 3:22,23 tells us another of the Father's qualities that you need to know: He has compassion on you every morning.

Through the Lord's mercies we are not consumed, because His compassions fail not. They are new every morning....

Every morning when you get up, your Heavenly Father is ready with new compassions to pour out on you. That is His will every morning — and it will *always* be His will because He is God, and He changes not (*see* Malachi 3:6). That is the heart of the Father toward you as His child.

The same is true for Jesus. In the New Testament, it says more than 20 times that Jesus had compassion. One example is found in Luke 7. I love this passage of Scripture because it shows us so beautifully the compassion of our Savior.

And when He came near the gate of the city, behold, a dead man was being carried out, the only son of his mother; and she was a widow. And a large crowd from the city was with her. When the Lord saw her, He had compassion on her and said to her....

Luke 7:12,13

There was a lot going on at this moment. Jesus was walking the streets of Capernaum when He encountered a funeral procession as He came near the city gate. There was the body of a dead young man being carried to his place of burial, and a crowd of people were following behind. But Jesus didn't focus on all of that; He saw the woman who was the young man's mother, and Jesus felt compassion for her.

Then He said to her, "'...Do not weep'"(v. 13). What a word to come from Jesus!

Oh, the compassion of our God! This is Jesus — He is the express image of the will of the Father, and He has the same compassion as the Father. And His compassion has not changed!

Is your heart broken today? Jesus absolutely has compassion for you right now. And that compassion is active, not passive.

Jesus didn't just look at this mother's situation and think, *Oh, this is so sad because this woman is a widow, and this young man was her only son, her only means of income. She might become a beggar. She's going to become dependent on society. Her life is going to greatly change. I'm so sorry for this woman.*

No, that's not what Jesus said. He simply looked at her and said, "Do not weep" — because He knew the miracle that was coming next!

> **Then He [Jesus] came and touched the open coffin, and those who carried him stood still. And He said, "Young man, I say to you, arise." So he who was dead sat up and began to speak. And He presented him to his mother.**
>
> **Luke 7:14,15**

Oh, that we could be so bold and led by the Spirit as Jesus! Friend, I believe the Holy Spirit is working in us to get us to this point!

What a powerful demonstration of the active compassion of our Lord Jesus Christ! And that was not only Jesus' will at that moment; it was also the will of the Father — and it is still the Father's will for us today. Resurrection life includes healing of broken hearts and deliverance from sickness afflicting our bodies with fear and tormenting pain. These are all part of the Father's compassions that Jesus purchased for us on the Cross and that are continually available in our lives. Our part is to receive and activate them in our lives by faith.

IN COMPASSION HE SAYS YES

In Matthew 8:2 and 3, we see again that it is the will of God to have compassion on us. He wants to heal our bodies; He wants us whole in every area of our lives. This passage speaks of a leprous man who knew that Jesus *could* heal him, but he didn't know if Jesus *wanted* to heal him.

And behold, a leper came and worshiped Him, saying, "Lord, if You are willing, You can make me clean." Then Jesus put out His hand and touched him, saying, "I am willing; be cleansed." Immediately his leprosy was cleansed.

We need to know what the will of God is regarding healing — and we see it in this verse. Jesus' will was to heal this leprous man.

Just consider the realities of this leprous man in the hours right before he met Jesus. When this man first opened his eyes that morning, it was just like any other morning. He didn't know that it was going to be his miracle morning. He got out of bed in his same old routine — carrying the same familiar burden of pain, shame, and fear and the same horrible identity as a leper that he had carried for years.

But this man had a burning question in his heart. He had heard about Jesus' healing the sick; he knew that Jesus was able to heal. Yet one thing he didn't know — would Jesus *want* to heal *him*?

So this leprous man was set up to experience a powerful reality that day: Jesus' absolute willingness to deliver and heal. At some point, the man decided to push past his fear and risk going out in public to find Jesus and ask Him the question burning in his heart: *"Are You willing to heal me?"*

Imagine what it was like for this man to push through the crowd with his body ravaged by leprosy. Everywhere he turned, people were backing away from him, yelling to each other, "Unclean! Unclean!" as they protected themselves from the horrible stench of this dreaded, contagious disease.

But, finally, the man reached Jesus. And when Jesus said to him, *"I am willing,"* Jesus' words became this man's place of faith. From that moment on, his faith rested on the reality of Jesus' willingness to heal *him. And the next reality that manifested was the answer this man had longed for!*

That morning this man got out of bed still leprous, but that evening he went to bed healed and made whole!

When we are confronted by the challenge of our present reality or circumstances, we must make a choice as to what we're going to believe and accept. The truth is, we can get so caught up in the physical realm and think, *I'm not going to live in denial. I need to be real about this problem.* It's true that symptoms present us with one version of reality. But what about our place of faith? Is that not a greater reality? Absolutely! And it leads to our answer becoming our *new* reality!

You may be facing a challenge, and perhaps you've been feeling trapped in the reality of that problem. But Jesus is inviting you to another place, the place called faith — because that is the reality that comes before your miracle! In that place of faith, Jesus is your Healer. You're not a believer in denial who does not face your circumstances — your present reality. You're simply walking in the place of faith. That place is where you abide *before* your answer or manifestation becomes your new reality.

When somebody believes, that's the reality of faith. Yes, the problem is one reality, but the answer to that problem is another reality. And between the two is the reality of faith that doesn't give up — faith that says, "I *am* going to receive from God, no question about it!"

The man who was about to be healed and delivered from leprosy didn't know that this was going to be his life-altering miracle day. He just made a decision to get out of bed, get dressed, and leave his home to go look for Jesus. But God was working a plan.

This man knew Jesus *could* heal, no problem. He had probably thought a lot about it before this moment: *I've heard of this Jesus performing miracles. I believe He can heal me — but does He want to heal me?* Then Jesus spoke three words to the man that settled that question once and for all: *"I am willing."*

So for this amazing miracle to happen, there were only two questions this man had to settle in his own mind: *Can Jesus do it? Yes, He can. And does He want to do it? Now I know — yes, He does.*

In that place of faith, Jesus is your Healer. You're not a believer in denial who does not face your circumstances — your present reality. You're simply walking in the place of faith. That place is where you abide *before* your answer or manifestation becomes your new reality.

IT IS *ALWAYS* GOD'S WILL
TO SEE YOU HEALED AND MADE WHOLE!

These are the same two questions we still ask today: *Can Jesus heal me?* and *Does He want to heal me?*

He is the God of the impossible! He most assuredly *can* heal you. And He is the same yesterday, today, and forever, so you can also know beyond a shadow of a doubt that today, He *wants* to heal you — just as He healed the leprous man that day almost 2,000 years ago!

Friend, I'm writing this to *you*. If you have sickness, pain, or disease — anything that's trying to attach itself to your body — the will of God absolutely is to heal you. *Can* He heal you? Yes, He is the God of the impossible! He most assuredly *can* heal you. And He is the same yesterday, today, and forever, so you can also know beyond a shadow of a doubt that today, He *wants* to heal you — just as He healed the leprous man that day almost 2,000 years ago!

If a sickness goes on for a long time, sometimes we start to believe religious statements like, *Well, maybe God doesn't really want to heal me. Maybe I'm giving glory to God through my patient suffering. Or maybe He wants to teach me something through this sickness.* But the answer to all three of those "maybe's" is *no, no,* and *no*. None of those statements reflects the true nature or the will of our Father God!

God doesn't want His children sick in order to teach them something. Sickness is ultimately from the devil and originates in this fallen world. So why would God use something from the devil to teach us anything? That doesn't make any sense, because the Bible says the devil is under our feet (*see* Ephesians 1:20-22; 2:6)!

Jesus defeated Satan through His death, burial, and resurrection, and that includes the defeat of every sickness the enemy brings! Jesus doesn't use Satan or his evil ways to teach us anything.

Does it bring glory to God when we suffer with sickness? No, Jesus took all our sicknesses and diseases on Himself as He hung on that Cross.

I'm telling you right now, any sickness or disease that is afflicting your body or tormenting your soul for any reason is not giving glory to God. This is such good news. Jesus took that physical or mental affliction to hell, and He punished it, forever destroying its power and its right to remain on you!

The truth is, Jesus hates sickness and disease. There is nothing in Him that loves seeing people being tormented or in pain or that enjoys watching people lose all their money because they have to pay doctors for medical care. That brings Him no joy. In fact, Jesus *hates* it — so much so that He offered Himself as a Sacrifice and suffered a horrifying death on the Cross to purchase our redemption and healing.

And even before Jesus was nailed to the Cross, He took that beating with a whip that had multiple cords with pieces of metal and glass tied on the ends. When those pieces of metal and glass came ripping through His body, they tore His flesh. The pain and torture Jesus endured during that cruel lashing of His flesh, muscles, and organs is unimaginable. Yet the Word says it was that very whipping that purchased our healing: "…By His stripes we are healed" (Isaiah 53:5).

Psalm 103:2,3 confirms to us what the Father's compassions and benefits include for us. He not only forgives *all* our sin; He also promises to heal our bodies of *all* sickness and disease.

Bless the Lord, O my soul, and forget not all His benefits: who forgives all your iniquities, who heals all your diseases.

It is absolutely God's will for you to be healed. It's as much God's will to *heal* you as it is to *save* you. His compassions are available right now for you. It's as if there were a basket in front of you labeled, "The Father's Compassions," and you could decide, *I'm going to reach into that basket and take out the compassion called healing, because Jesus is the same yesterday, today, and forever, and that healing is mine.*

I personally have been touched by Jesus' healing power so many times in my life. That's why I minister this truth that He bore our sicknesses and diseases with so much passion and gratitude. His healing, miracle-working power is absolutely paid for and available, ready for *you* to receive right now.

Friend, there is nothing in the will of God that wants you sick or in pain — *nothing*.

And as I told you earlier, the Father's compassions have already been poured out. They are yours for the taking! The will of God was to heal the leper, and the will of God is to heal *you*.

When Jesus said on the Cross, *"It is finished,"* He was saying, "I have just paid for cancer, for arthritis, for mental illness, for lung problems, for skin disease, for blood problems, for kidney disease. I have just paid for anything wrong with your sinuses, your throat, or your ears. I have just paid for blindness. *I have just paid for it all. IT IS FINISHED!*"

At the very moment Jesus spoke those words, "*It is finished,*" the veil was torn that protected the Holy of Holies. In that split second, the presence of God moved out of the manmade Temple to live inside human flesh and blood, and provision was made for our salvation and healing.

Hebrews 12:2 says that Jesus endured the Cross, despising the shame for the joy set before Him. That joy was a demonstration of everything He was paying a price for to free us from sin and sickness.

Yes, it is Jesus' *joy* to heal you. Always remember this, for healing is a huge part of your amazing, wonderful, great salvation!

At the very moment Jesus spoke those words, "*It is finished,*" the veil was torn that protected the Holy of Holies. In that split second, the presence of God moved out of the manmade Temple to live inside human flesh and blood, and provision was made for our salvation and healing.

GOD'S PERFECT PLAN TO RESCUE YOU

Here's something else you must never forget: Your great salvation wasn't your idea. You didn't get good enough to receive Jesus. You didn't choose Him — He chose *you*. It was His idea to save you. It was His idea to arrange circumstances in your life so you would hear the Gospel, repent of your ways, and turn to Him. It was His plan of rescue from eternal damnation for you — a plan prepared before the foundation of the world (*see* Revelation 13:8).

Isn't that powerful? God loves us so much that He came up with the amazing, restoring, rescuing plan of a Savior for us! He saw our lost condition; He saw that we were sinners. We had messed up. We had fallen short and missed the glory of God (*see* Romans 3:23). So the Father sent His only Son, and when the time came, He put all our sin and sickness on Him so that after Jesus paid the full price as our Sacrificial Lamb, we could have a relationship with the Father.

The moment we received Jesus as our Savior, we received a deposit on the inside — a guarantee or down payment for our eternal salvation, assuring us that when we die, we'll go straight to Heaven. That deposit is the Holy Spirit. He came to dwell within us the moment we were born again.

In Him you also trusted, after you heard the word of truth, the gospel of your salvation; in whom also, having believed, you were sealed with the Holy Spirit of promise, who is the guarantee of our inheritance until the redemption of the purchased possession, to the praise of His glory.

Ephesians 1:13,14

When that heavenly down payment called the Holy Spirit came to dwell within you, He gave you a sign in the spirit realm that read, "I don't belong to myself. I don't belong to this world. I belong to Him. My life is not my own. My life is *His*."

Along with the Holy Spirit, you received the gift of righteousness at the moment of your new birth. We read in Second Corinthians 5:21 that Jesus, who knew no sin, became sin so that you could become the righteousness of God in Him. That is such a powerful truth.

And as we have been discussing, another blessing in this magnificent salvation package is *healing*. This isn't healing when you go to Heaven. The Bible says there won't be any suffering in Heaven (*see* Revelation 21:4). Therefore, there will be no need for healing there. No, God's promise of healing is for while you're here on earth. It is a gift to you through the Father's great plan of salvation.

THE REALITY BEHIND THE PHRASE 'BY HIS STRIPES'

I want to share an excerpt from my husband Rick's book, *Paid in Full*. In this book, Rick talks about the scourging Jesus received. The Bible says that it was those stripes, those terrible wounds inflicted all over Jesus' body, that paid for our healing.

In Matthew 27:26, it says that the Roman governor, Pontius Pilate, "...released Barabbas to them; and when he had *scourged Jesus*, he delivered Him to be crucified." That phrase "scourged Jesus" is just two words, but as you read the following description of what a Roman scourging entailed, you will see the magnitude of those two small words.

This was considered to be one of the most feared and deadly weapons of the Roman world. It was so ghastly that the mere threat of scourging could calm a crowd or bend the will of the strongest rebel. Even the most hardened criminal recoiled from the prospect of being submitted to the vicious beating of a Roman scourge.

Most often, two torturers were utilized to carry out this punishment, simultaneously lashing the victim from both sides. As these dual whips struck the victim, the leather straps with their sharp, jagged objects descended and extended over his entire back. Each piece of metal, wire, bone, or glass cut deeply through the victim's skin and into his flesh, shredding his muscles and sinews.

Every time the whip pounded across the victim, those straps of leather curled tortuously around his torso, biting painfully and deeply into the skin of his abdomen and upper chest. As each stroke lacerated the sufferer, he tried to thrash about but was unable to move because his wrists were held so firmly to the metal ring above his head. Helpless to escape the whip, he would scream for mercy that this anguish might come to an end.[1]

We don't know that Jesus screamed for mercy, but we know that He endured this torturous beating. Isaiah 53:5 says that "...by His stripes we are healed." But in First Peter 2:24, where Peter quoted Isaiah 53:5, he told his readers, "...by whose stripes you *were* healed" — past tense.

In Rick's book *Paid in Full*, he wrote that the Greek word for "stripes" that is used in this verse describes *a full-body bruise* and "...refers to *a terrible lashing that draws blood and that produces discoloration and swelling of the entire body.*"[2]

Peter, the apostle who wrote those words in First Peter 2:24, actually saw what happened to Jesus at the whipping post. You and I weren't there; we didn't see this, but we read about it in Scripture. Now it is our opportunity and our great privilege to believe the Word of God and say, "This verse wasn't written just

---

[1] Rick Renner, *Paid in Full* (Tulsa, OK: Teach All Nations, 2008), p. 171.
[2] Ibid., p. 173.

for me to feel guilty whenever I'm dealing with pain or sickness in my body. Jesus did this so I could be *free* of the pain and the symptoms that are afflicting my body right now!"

How can we not focus on Jesus and all that He went through for us? Every drop of Jesus' blood had our name on it. And the more we gaze upon Him, the more we will want to know Him — and the more we will desire not to allow what He gave so freely to have happened in vain.

> Every drop of Jesus' blood had our name on it. And the more we gaze upon Him, the more we will want to know Him — and the more we will desire not to allow what He gave so freely to have happened in vain.

I personally don't yet have the full revelation of all that Jesus purchased for me as He bore those stripes on His back. But the question set before me is the same one set before every child of God: Am I going to just read and memorize Scripture about His redemptive work on my behalf, or will I receive healing as my inheritance and begin to walk in divine health by faith?

2

~

OUR SAVIOR *AND* OUR HEALER!

Jesus didn't endure that scourging in vain. He took those stripes so we would place our faith in what He did for us and receive our healing. But we have to *believe* it.

Why would Jesus willingly subject Himself to such horrible treatment? Because it was His Father's will, and it was also *Jesus'* will to free you from suffering and torment. Jesus' will and the Father's will are 100 percent the same — *the same in purpose, the same in plan, and the same in power.*

We can't separate healing from Jesus' character, from His purpose, or from His heart. Healing is not just one of Jesus' functions — that is absolutely who He *is*. He is a Healer and a Deliverer. His very name is Jehovah-Rapha, which

We can't separate healing from Jesus' character, from His purpose, or from His heart. Healing is not just one of Jesus' functions — that is absolutely who He *is*.

means "the God who heals," and how can you separate any person from his name?

We have to come to the place where *we know that we know* that *Healer* is precisely who Jesus is and that it's His will to heal *us*. Jesus is no less our Healer than He is our Savior.

HIS POWER SAVES *AND* HEALS!

Do you remember what Jesus said to the paralyzed man whose friends lowered him through the ceiling (*see* Luke 5:17-26)? He said, "...Man, your sins are forgiven you" (v. 20).

The Pharisees got upset, protesting, "You can't do that — only God can forgive sin!" (*see* v. 21).

But Jesus, completely unruffled, replied, "Which is easier, to say, 'Your sins are forgiven you,' or to say, 'Rise up and walk'?" (v. 23).

> **"But that you may know that the Son of Man has power on earth to forgive sins" — He said to the man who was paralyzed, "I say to you, arise, take up your bed, and go to your house." Immediately he rose up before them, took up what he had been lying on, and departed to his own house, glorifying God.**
>
> **Luke 5:24,25**

In that moment, Jesus was both saying and demonstrating, "You can't see that this man's sins have been forgiven him, but it is done. I will now do something that you *can* see — he will rise up and walk! But one is not greater than the other. I am both Savior *and* Healer."

The Pharisees didn't believe Jesus had the authority to forgive sins, because only God has that authority. So to demonstrate His authority, Jesus healed the man — revealing in that miraculous act that the same divine power, coming from the same Source, both heals *and* forgives!

IDENTIFYING WITH THE GREAT PHYSICIAN

Just as Jesus was willing to die for our salvation, He was willing to endure that horrible scourging to heal us and keep us whole while we're on this earth.

Jesus knew what Isaiah 53:5 says. He knew that the stripes He received were the necessary price He had to pay for our healing. He could have just gone to the Cross to purchase our salvation and avoided the pain of that scourging. Certainly in Jesus' humanity, He didn't want to endure the added torture. But He knew that the redemption of mankind wouldn't be complete without including man's physical healing — so He submitted to the scourging just as He later laid down His life to be hung on that Cross.

> **"Therefore My Father loves Me, because I lay down My life that I may take it again. No one takes it from Me, but I lay it down of Myself. I have power to lay it down, and I have power to take it again. This command I have received from My Father."**
>
> **John 10:17,18**

Jesus' power to heal is the same as His power to save, because it is all the testimony of the power in His precious blood. Our minds have to get renewed to that truth so we don't struggle with this thought when our bodies are hurting. Jesus wants us to receive our healing as simply as we received our salvation.

I believe we often see salvation and healing as two separate operations because we view situations carnally. We feel symptoms; we see physical issues. We're bombarded by media, by commercials, by other people's opinions. We see people around us identifying with sickness, making it their own: "Oh, I need to go to the doctor! I've got this symptom. I've got this pain." Yet here we are with the message of Christ — the Solution. All that is left is for us to identify with who He already is in us: "He is my Healer. He already bore my sickness so I don't have to bear or carry it any longer!"

> Jesus' power to heal is the same as His power to save, because it is all the testimony of the power in His precious blood.

Of course, a person can be healed and still be lost and go to hell — or he can be sick in his body, yet be saved and go to Heaven. So getting saved is eternal and, in that sense, it is greater. But Jesus' power to save someone is the same power He has to heal that person!

Jesus *is* the Great Physician! And although we're thankful for doctors, Jesus is in a class all by Himself. He isn't "practicing medicine."

That's how we describe our doctors — as those who practice medicine. No matter how good our doctors are, they are limited in their knowledge, and they are, in a sense, practicing on us. But Jesus does not "practice medicine." He comes with His laser-sharp power to cut out whatever is afflicting our bodies at the source and eliminate its destructive effects once and for all!

But everything I've been telling you to this point has to come by revelation. You can hear it all day long in your mind; you can say it out of your mouth. But if you don't come to the place where you believe it — where you know that you *know* it's true — you'll miss out on experiencing the reality of Jesus as your Healer when sickness tries to attack your body.

Make God's Voice Louder
Than the Voice of Your Pain

I have received healing in my life at different times, and I found each time that there was a need to seek God and to *keep on* seeking Him, to resist the enemy's lies and to *keep on* resisting them. Why is such a persistent focus on "things above" so necessary (*see* Colossians 3:2)? Because sickness has a way of speaking, and pain has a voice.

Sickness and pain will try to tell you:

- *"You're going to have this ailment for the rest of your life."*

- *"You're probably going to die an early death."*

- *"Maybe Jesus doesn't really want to heal you of this. Maybe He's trying to teach you something through suffering."*

Oh, yes, sickness and pain have a voice — so we have to set our hearts and our ears to listen to God and to say only what *He* says. When you hear His voice (and His voice can clearly be heard in His Word), you hear His will.

The Holy Spirit will never speak contrary to the Word, or the will, of the Father. So if you know what the Word of God says or you know the Holy Spirit has spoken to your spirit, you can take it to the bank: You have just heard the will of the Father for you, and I'm telling you, He says, *Yes, you are healed!"*

I love that, because the Father is saying those words to *you*; He's not talking to ten other people. He's so individual — as if you were the only one Jesus came to die for. And even if you were the only one, Jesus would have taken the scourging so you could be healed.

I have received healing in my life at different times, and I found each time that there was a need to seek God and to *keep on* seeking Him, to resist the enemy's lies and to *keep on* resisting them. Why is such a persistent focus on "things above" so necessary? Because sickness has a way of speaking, and pain has a voice.

Jesus already suffered to pay the price for your healing. Your only "suffering" should be in the effort required of you to resist every attack of the enemy against your body. And you have to speak out loud to resist his assaults against your body *and* your mind. Speak back at the enemy's attack!

You can say: "Devil, in the name of Jesus, you're not going to do this. I know what the Word of God says!"

There is real pressure brought against you in this process of believing and receiving anything that God freely gives you. When fear and pain and perhaps a doctor's report of a life-threatening illness are speaking — when something is threatening your physical comfort and your overall well-being — it can be difficult to sustain the fight of faith.

Remember, you have to keep speaking back! Drown out those opposing voices with the truth of God's Word coming out of your mouth! Declare, "Jesus bore this sickness and pain, so I position myself to seek Him and to do whatever I need to do to get to the place where I truly believe what He did for me and that healing is already mine!"

Healing is available for every single person, but it takes this kind of offensive positioning to withstand the attack when the enemy is trying to steal, kill, and destroy. Satan knows he doesn't have much time, and he's trying to escalate his attacks and cause as many casualties as possible in his war against righteousness.

So if you find yourself in the middle of a physical battle, whose voice will speak the loudest in *your* life? Will you take an immovable stance that you are going to finish your course, or are you going to allow it to be aborted prematurely by one of the enemy's tactics?

Think of the apostle Paul. If anyone had an opportunity to be sick, it was Paul! Think of all the infection that must have tried to attack his body throughout his years of ministry! And what about trauma?

> If you find yourself in the middle of a physical battle, whose voice will speak the loudest in *your* life? Will you take an immovable stance that you are going to finish your course, or are you going to allow it to be aborted prematurely by one of the enemy's tactics?

Over Paul's years of ministry, he was shipwrecked, stoned, beaten, and left for dead (*see* 2 Corinthians 11:25). What kind of wounds were inflicted on Paul's body that required him to fight the good fight of faith in order to receive his healing?

Yet the apostle Paul didn't die sick. He didn't die rejected. He didn't die sad. And he didn't die unwilling! God's voice was always the loudest in Paul's life, no matter what. And when the time came, he simply said, "It's the appointed time for my departure. I have finished my race" (*see* 2 Timothy 4:6,7).

SPIRITUAL PROTOCOL
IN GOD'S THRONE ROOM

God doesn't want us to come to Him and beg for our healing. Hebrews 4:16 tells us that we are to come *boldly* before His throne. But let's look at the verse that comes right before that one to get a better understanding of what He is telling us.

> **For we do not have a High Priest who cannot sympathize with our weaknesses, but was in all points tempted as we are, yet without sin.**
>
> **Hebrews 4:15**

God knows that we are weak; He knows that we are made of dust. He understands why we get fearful at times when sickness comes on our bodies. He understands why we might doubt, because His Son was tempted in all the same ways.

Now let's look at the next verse, which reveals the will of God for us.

> **Let us therefore come boldly to the throne of grace, that we may obtain mercy and find grace to help in time of need.**
>
> **Hebrews 4:16**

So you don't just come into God's presence because it's your religious duty. You approach the throne of grace because that is the place to come to receive mercy and find grace to help you in your time of need.

And God says to come *boldly*. That means to enter His presence with a forthrightness that says, "Father, I am Your child, and I believe that You hear me. I believe that Your Son Jesus was tempted in the same way I was, yet He didn't sin. I receive Your forgiveness for my fear and my doubt, and I'm coming boldly to Your throne to receive what is already mine through Jesus. And this is what I want on this visit to Your throne!"

What is it you want from the Lord? Be bold! If it is healing and wholeness, tell Him, "Father, this is what I want!" That is exactly what Hebrews 4:16 is telling us to do. We are to come boldly to the throne of grace and receive our Heavenly Father's mercy to help us in our time of need.

We have to see this! It's not a religious duty — it's our life in God. And it's not just for someone else — it's for you and for me!

JESUS ALREADY BORE
EVERY SICKNESS AND DISEASE

When Jesus was on the earth, He preached, taught about, and demonstrated the power of God. He healed so many people and performed so many miracles during His brief time of ministry on the earth that John wrote in his gospel that the world itself wouldn't have room for the books that could be written to describe them all (*see* John 21:25)!

But Jesus doesn't want us to know Him as the Miracle Worker just by reading about it in the Bible. He doesn't want us just to enjoy a moment of "mental assent" about who He is because we heard about Him and agreed, saying, "Oh, yes, Jesus is the Healer." He doesn't want us just to have *head knowledge* with no expectation in our heart for Him to heal us personally.

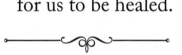

> Jesus doesn't want us to know Him far away — He wants us to know Him close up! He wants us to *experience* His healing power. That's why He paid such a heavy price for us to be healed.

Jesus wants us to *experience* Him as the Miracle Worker in our own lives. He is a personal God. Jesus doesn't want us to know Him far away — He wants us to know Him close up! He wants us to *experience* His healing power. That's why He paid such a heavy price for us to be healed.

Hundreds of years before Jesus walked this earth and died on the Cross as the perfect Sacrifice, it was prophesied that He was going to bear our sicknesses and our pain. Isaiah 53:4 says, "Surely he has borne our griefs and carried our sorrows...." That word "griefs" really means *sicknesses*. It goes on to say, "...Yet we esteemed Him stricken, smitten by God, and afflicted."

What was Jesus afflicted with? With every sickness and disease that would ever try to come on you and me. It all came on Him first. He carried every pain and every sickness to the Cross so we wouldn't have to carry them!

In the hours leading up to Calvary and as Jesus hung on the Cross, there was so much of His blood spilled and so much ripping of His flesh that He became unrecognizable. The Bible actually says He didn't even look like a man (*see* Isaiah 52:14)! But it was all part of Jesus' taking all our sin and all our sicknesses and infirmities on His own body so that we can live free from all that kept us bound under Satan's dominion.

What a Savior — what a plan!

3

~

THE POWER OF OUR
TESTIMONY

The Bible says in Revelation 12:11 that our testimony is so powerful, it defeats the devil. When we hear people's testimonies of miracles that they've experienced, it builds our faith to believe God for more miracles!

I have a TV program in Russia and America designed to minister to both men and women. On my program, I'm always talking about miracles and the power of God in demonstration because I've seen so many miracles in other people's lives, and Jesus has done so many miracles in my own life.

To encourage your faith, I'll share one of the testimonies I received from a viewer of my program. This woman had contracted COVID and was experiencing pain throughout her body. One night she was in so much pain that she wasn't able to sleep at all. The next Sunday, this woman was watching a Moscow Good News Church service online, and she heard me instruct all who were in pain to stand up and raise their hands as I prepared to pray for them.

The woman stood up and raised her hands there in her home. And as I began to pray for healing, her pain completely disappeared, never to come back! By faith this woman had received the healing that was already hers from the Healer who had already paid the price!

> By faith this woman had received the healing that was already hers from the Healer who had already paid the price!

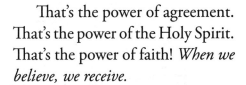

That's the power of agreement. That's the power of the Holy Spirit. That's the power of faith! *When we believe, we receive.*

That is what happened to this woman. She believed on Jesus, the One who had already borne all her sickness and disease! And she received the manifestation of healing in her body — right there in her home!

IT'S MY TURN TO TESTIFY!

I know this about Jesus: He *is* the Miracle Worker. He *is* the Healer.

But can I be honest with you? I didn't start out like that. My faith grew as I sought my God when problems arose, and again and again, He would perform a miracle in my life. He would bring healing; He would bring deliverance; He would bring peace.

Today I can't help but preach about the power in the stripes of Jesus both to heal and deliver us, because I've been healed again and again and have received miracles in my own life. A little further in the book, I'll share the testimony of the first healing miracle I experienced in my twenties, which marked the beginning of my journey in learning about Jesus as my Healer. But for now, let me share a couple of other personal testimonies of healing that I experienced a little later down the road of life.

When I was pregnant with our first son Paul, I felt so nauseous that I would often throw up any food that was in my stomach. I was, however, able to take some medicine that helped me get through that difficult period of my pregnancy.

But later when I was carrying Philip, our second son, I dealt with similar spells of intense nausea, to the point that I couldn't even keep water down. But this time, the medicine I'd taken before wasn't available. The doctor suggested another medicine that seemed to help settle my stomach, so I started taking it. But then Rick began teaching on Jesus our Healer. During each session, I listened intently, and suddenly a revelation of Isaiah 53:4 hit my heart — that Jesus actually *took* my sicknesses.

One night I prayed, "God, since Jesus took my sickness, I don't have to take it. He took it for me, so why should I bear it? I know I'm depending on this medicine. And I see that Jesus is my Healer. So tonight I'm not taking my medicine, because Jesus already took my pains and my sicknesses."

I'm not telling you to stop taking your medicine, nor am I even suggesting that. This was simply *my* step of faith.

At this point during my pregnancy, I was in my sixth month of getting sick if I didn't take the medicine. As I said previously, before this particular night, I would get so nauseous that I couldn't even keep water down, so my deciding not to take my medicine was a real step of faith.

I went to bed that night and woke up at three o'clock in the morning, sick to my stomach. But I said, "No, I'm not going to take this nausea — because Jesus already took it. I'm taking my healing!" I lay there and quoted the Word. With Isaiah 53:4, I fought against my sickness!

I *knew* I had my answer. I went back to sleep — and the next morning, I was completely healed! From that time on, I never had another symptom of nausea. And I didn't take that medicine anymore — because I had gotten a revelation of the truth that Jesus had *surely* borne my sickness, so I didn't have to!

Because of experiences like this, Isaiah 53 was no longer just words written in the Bible; it was truth for me *personally*. I took Jesus at His Word. I said to Him, "You took my sicknesses, so I'm not taking them" — and He completely healed me!

This is why I so passionately want people to see that Jesus is the Healer — because I've experienced Him as *my* Healer. Even to look at my physical surroundings and see them clearly is a miracle in my life performed by Jesus my Healer. Over the past few years, I've experienced a gradual but dramatic improvement in my eyesight — and I wasn't even believing God for it!

I wasn't believing God to specifically heal my eyes, but I *was* seeking Him. And Hebrews 11:6 says, "…Without faith it is impossible to please Him, for he who comes to God must believe that He is, *and that He is a rewarder of those who diligently seek Him.*" Although we can't earn His blessings, we can cooperate with Him and His Word and receive the benefits of our cooperation. And I believe the healing in my eyes was a reward from the Lord according to Hebrews 11:6.

Let me share with you how this happened. Several times over the past few years, I'd begun to not see well through my contact lenses. So I'd make an appointment with my optometrist, and each time he'd say, "Your eyes are improving. That's why you can't see through your contacts," and he would give me new contacts with lesser strength or correction. Then one day he told me, "One of your eyes has improved so much that you don't need a contact in that eye any longer!"

When I heard that, I said to the Lord in my heart, *Lord, I just praise You. You're a Rewarder, and You know I've been diligently seeking You.*

I also had this thought later when pondering the gradual healing of my eyes that is still in process: When we sit in the corporate anointing among other believers and the Holy Spirit is present and working among us, we simply don't know all that He is doing. But in every service, no matter where I am, I always say, "Lord, whatever You're doing right now, I open myself to receive it."

I know He honors hearts that diligently seek Him. That place of seeking is a place in Him that He has called us to abide in. Healing is in that place, because He *wants* to heal us.

I don't know if it was in this kind of public setting that God worked on my eyes, but I know He honors hearts that diligently seek Him. That place of seeking is a place in Him that He has called us to abide in. Healing is in that place, because He *wants* to heal us.

The more you seek God, the closer He draws to you, and He shows you who He is. So don't let yourself get discouraged — just keep believing. Keep hungering for Him, reading God's Word, and listening to good teaching about His miracle-working power. Keep listening to people's testimonies of how God miraculously healed and delivered them. Keep diligently seeking Him!

HOPE WHEN THERE SEEMS TO BE NO HOPE

I understand that it can be a challenge at times not to let yourself get discouraged when an ailment or condition goes on for a long time and it seems like there is no answer. I want to share a testimony along this line to show you how God can turn around the most hopeless-looking, long-term situation in a person's life by the power of His Spirit.

My heart was so impacted when I heard this testimony of a woman who spent most of her life experiencing terrible rejection. She was born into a situation where the grownups in her life hated her and didn't want her alive. They left her for dead when she was a little girl, and she did almost die. But a woman walking by heard her crying and saved this little girl's life.

That may sound like a story with a great ending. But after this precious girl was rescued from death at that young age, over the decades that followed, she continued to find herself in situations in which she was rejected again and again. Finally, when this woman was in her 80s, she lost her mind.

But the Lord had placed in this afflicted woman's life a Christian woman who knew how to pray, and He spoke to this Christian lady's heart, *"I want you to baptize her."* The Christian woman obeyed the Lord — and as the old woman came back up out of the water, her mind was instantly restored to normal — a miracle!

What had occurred in the mind and emotions of this older woman looked like a hopeless situation. But through prayer and the obedience of one of God's children, this woman who had lived such a horrible life was saved, baptized, and restored in her mind — and she now lives in Heaven for eternity!

In Jesus, there is *always* hope, even when there seems to be no hope. He is our miracle-working God!

WHY ARE SOME NOT HEALED?

We've seen why we can know beyond a shadow of a doubt that it *is* the will of both the Father and Jesus that we walk in divine health. With that settled, how do we process the question, "Why is it that some very good Christians end up going into eternity without being healed?" How are we to understand this?

First, it's simply true that there are a lot of factors that we don't understand in particular situations. (But we know it's not because God didn't do His part; He isn't holding back on anyone's healing.) For one thing, people may have ways of thinking or dealing with situations in life that hinder them from receiving their healing.

For example, maybe they are secretly condemned in their heart about something that happened in their lives long ago. The enemy built a stronghold of condemnation in their heart and mind that they never dealt with, and it hindered their faith from operating.

Or maybe the person who is physically afflicted was wounded by others in life, and he or she never let that offense go. As a result, the person's unforgiveness opened the door for sickness to come and to stay.

We simply don't know what is in the hearts of the people involved.

The Bible says it's even difficult to know our own heart (*see* Jeremiah 17:9). I came to realize this about myself during my journey that led to my first experience of receiving a miraculous healing.

I suffered for 13 years from a terrible skin condition on my face and neck from the time I was 12 years old. (I tell my full testimony in Rick's and my autobiography *Unlikely* and in my book *Redeemed From Shame*.) The sores produced by the disease went through the five layers of my skin. It was painful and terribly embarrassing. As a young woman, I was turned down from jobs and singing opportunities because of the appearance of my face.

Even after I received the revelation years later that Jesus is my Healer, my healing didn't just instantly manifest. But as I kept confessing God's Word over a period of time, there came a powerful moment when the Holy Spirit showed me something in my heart that was hindering my healing. Up until that time, I didn't know that there even *was* a roadblock that could keep my healing from manifesting. I was simply standing on God's Word, and as I walked in the light of His truth, He showed me this roadblock.

All through my teens, I had to go to the doctor on a regular basis because of this skin condition. My mom spent large sums of money on doctors to try to help me. I took a great amount of medicine over the years, but the medicines and treatments didn't work for me; I just got worse.

These continual visits to the doctor gave me time to spend with my mother, and I enjoyed her attention. Even as horrible as the treatments were — having to endure the side effects of pain, blistering, and scaling — I still enjoyed those times of being with my mom and all the attention I received from her.

"Well, that's normal," some might say.

But fast forward to years later when I was 25 years old. The Lord showed me something important about my attachment to the attention I was getting from my mother.

But first let me tell you how hope, faith, and expectation came to my heart concerning healing and deliverance from my hopeless condition. You see, until that time, I simply thought it was my lot in life to suffer with this chronic skin condition. I assumed that it was up to me to find a way to adapt and make the best of it. I had no hope for anything better. I had even resorted to buying very expensive, thick makeup to camouflage the disease.

I hadn't yet come to the revelation that Jesus bore my sicknesses on the Cross. I didn't know He was my Healer. But that all changed one day as I just "happened" to come across a radio preacher teaching on healing. And as I listened to him teach, *there was a moment when hope came alive in my heart* as I heard him say from Isaiah 53:5, "By the stripes of Jesus, you are healed!"

When I heard that, I said to the Lord, "You mean that I can actually be *healed* after suffering from this condition for 13 years?"

It was in that moment that hope entered my heart and my journey of healing started. It wasn't the kind of hope that says, "Well, I sure *hope* I'll get healed." It was the kind of hope that is based on the Word and is full of expectation that the manifestation of my healing was surely in my future and that it was possible!

At that time, I knew very, very little about the principle of confessing the Word. I just did it because the radio preacher I was listening to said it was important.

When we start speaking God's Word out loud, something starts happening inside us. I knew so little at the time that I couldn't say, "My mind is changing on this subject of divine healing as I speak His Word!" Nonetheless, from the moment hope entered my heart, I started to faithfully confess God's promises in His Word and believe Him for my healing, and the power of His Word was doing a work in me.

> From the moment hope entered my heart, I started to faithfully confess God's promises in His Word and believe Him for my healing, and the power of His Word was doing a work in me.

Weeks passed, and I didn't see any difference in my outward appearance or feel any different. But as I focused on and confessed what the Word says about Jesus being my Healer, something was surely changing in me. I was changing from the inside out.

THE HOLY SPIRIT IS THE REVEALER OF OUR HEARTS

Then one day as I was sitting in my car, listening to a woman radio preacher teach on healing, she asked a question that was a *key* in my journey. It unlocked a door to my heart and allowed me to see what was inside.

The radio preacher asked, "Do you really *want* to be healed?" When she said that, the Holy Spirit made it personal and asked *me* that question. And as He did, He revealed what was in my heart. He showed me that I had enjoyed to a wrong degree the attention I had gotten from my mom because of the sickness.

As I mentioned earlier, Jeremiah 17:9 tells us that in ourselves, we can't truly know what is in our own hearts. But the Holy Spirit is a Revealer. He reveals the secret things that are binding us and the things that can set us free (*see* Daniel 2:22)!

The desire for my mother's attention had been binding me to the skin disease that had afflicted me for so long, but until that moment, I'd had no idea. I only could have discovered that by the Holy Spirit. And when He spoke those words into my heart through that radio preacher, the knowledge of what I had to do for deliverance also came. I immediately repented.

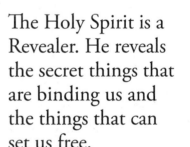

The Holy Spirit is a Revealer. He reveals the secret things that are binding us and the things that can set us free.

I prayed right then and there, "Lord, I don't want any more attention because of this condition. I want to be healed!"

As I sat in the car that day, there was just something about the delivering voice of the Holy Spirit speaking to my spirit through this radio preacher. I didn't have to wonder if the preacher's words applied to me. *I knew they did.*

Suddenly I understood something that I hadn't known about myself before that moment. That is the revealing power of the

Holy Spirit! And in that moment of revelation, I immediately dealt with the hindrance to my healing that the Holy Spirit had shown me.

Still, for the next several weeks after that experience, I didn't see any change in the skin disease. In fact, two months had gone by since the revelation of Isaiah 53:4,5 first dropped into my heart. Judging by what my situation looked like on the outside, I wasn't getting any better. Nevertheless, I believed that God was working, and I stayed in faith and kept doing what I knew to do — confessing what the Word says about my healing.

> Judging by what my situation looked like on the outside, I wasn't getting any better. Nevertheless, I believed that God was working, and I stayed in faith and kept doing what I knew to do — confessing what the Word says about my healing.

Then one night I went to bed with that disease, just as I had every other night for 13 years — but when I woke up the next morning, *I had received a complete miracle.* My forehead, my cheeks, and my neck were clear — the disease was completely gone!

Why did that happen? What freed me from that disease? That miracle happened because of the scourging of our Savior! Jesus didn't take that scourging in vain. He took those stripes so we would believe on what He did for us and receive our healing. But we have to *believe* it.

That's what happened in my situation. First, I believed God's Word. And when the Holy Spirit's delivering voice through that woman radio preacher revealed to me the hindrance to my healing, I immediately responded and He dealt with it. Then in the weeks that followed, somehow as I saw His words with my eyes, spoke His words with my mouth, and heard His words with my ears, the power of those words made their way into my heart. And at some moment when my heart came into complete agreement with the words I was speaking, I was healed.

Why would Jesus willingly subject Himself to such horrible treatment? Because it was His Father's will to free you from suffering and torment. Jesus' will and the Father's will are 100 percent the same — same in purpose, same in plan, same in power.

So I can boldly proclaim — and so can you: Jesus *is* my Healer! God is faithful, and His promises are true!

As I saw His words with my eyes, spoke His words with my mouth, and heard His words with my ears, the power of those words made their way into my heart. And at some moment when my heart came into complete agreement with the words I was speaking, I was healed.

4

~

THE DELIVERING VOICE OF GOD

In my journey of healing that I just shared with you, there came a pivotal moment that released Heaven's answer into my situation. The radio preacher's question — "Do you really want to be healed?" — wasn't just a question posed by a natural man. It was the voice of the Holy Spirit speaking straight to my heart through one of God's servants for my deliverance.

There is such power in the delivering voice of God! When He speaks and we respond, His voice takes precedence over what we think and what we're going through. It simply becomes a matter of, *"We're done here — I'm free."* It's the word we *hear* and *believe* that changes everything.

OLD TESTAMENT EXAMPLES

Consider Jacob. He was on a journey that took him from being called Jacob, which means *the supplanter*, to receiving a new name, Israel, meaning *prince with God* or *prevailed with God*.

During that journey, Jacob's heart was already turning toward God. Jacob was praying, but he was still on his way to his destination (*see* Genesis 32:9-12). He sent everyone ahead who was traveling with him, and he was left alone.

> There is such power in the delivering voice of God! When He speaks and we respond, His voice takes precedence over what we think and what we're going through. It simply becomes a matter of, *"We're done here — I'm free."* It's the word we *hear* and *believe* that changes everything.

I encourage you to read this account in Genesis. Jacob was en route to meet his brother, whom he had supplanted and undermined in order to receive the blessing of the birthright of the firstborn — and the firstborn was Esau, *not* Jacob.

But that night a Man wrestled with Jacob all through the night. Afterward, the Man spoke, changing Jacob's name to Israel because he had contended with God and prevailed. That was the delivering voice of God, and that voice completely changed Jacob into another man (*see* Genesis 32:22-30).

What about Moses? The same delivering voice of God came to Moses when he was a shepherd in the desert and saw a burning bush. God's voice came out of that bush, and on the other side of that experience, Moses was changed to another man (*see* Exodus 3 and 4).

And think of Gideon. The angel of the Lord said, *"Gideon, you're a mighty warrior of valor!"*

Gideon answered, "No, I'm only the least one in the least clan of Manasseh" (*see* Judges 6:12,15).

But the voice of God prevailed, and the power of that voice delivered Gideon into the position of a mighty warrior — shifting him into an entirely new identity that was required to fulfill his destiny (*see* Judges 7).

Now think of Rahab. All she heard was people's talk about the great victories the God of Israel had wrought for His people. But Rahab believed those words, and, as a result, those words became the delivering voice of God to her and her family.

Rahab acted on the truth she had heard and risked her life to help God's people — and, as a result, their lives were spared (*see* Joshua 2 and 6). And in the end, she not only found a new home and a new people, but later Rahab was also given the honor of becoming a mother in the lineage of the future Messiah (*see* Matthew 1:5)!

NEW TESTAMENT EXAMPLES

Then in the New Testament, we see the example of blind Bartimaeus. He also knew about the delivering voice of God (*see* Mark 10:46-52). When he heard that Jesus was walking by, he started calling out to the Master, "Son of David, have mercy on me!" The crowd told him to be quiet, but Bartimaeus cried out all the more.

Then Jesus stopped and said, "Call him here!" The fickle crowd changed their tune and started telling Bartimaeus, "Cheer up! Jesus is calling for you!"

That was all Bartimaeus needed to hear. He threw off his cloak, which identified him as a blind beggar, and made his way toward the sound of Jesus' voice. Bartimaeus was as good as seeing before he ever reached Jesus! The blind man *knew* he was about to receive a miracle, just from the sound of the delivering voice of the Master!

> The blind man *knew* he was about to receive a miracle, just from the sound of the delivering voice of the Master!

And think of the woman who suffered with an issue of blood for so many years (*see* Mark 5:25-34). We'll talk more about her in the next chapter, but for now, let's focus on the delivering voice of God in this woman's life.

The Bible says this woman had "heard" something (*see* Mark 5:27). She had probably heard someone say, "Jesus healed me!" or, "Jesus healed my loved one!" The talk that had been circulating of Jesus as the Healer is how she even knew to begin her journey.

This woman may have also heard that a man, once lame, was now walking or that a demon-possessed child had been delivered. She may have heard that a blind man who had been blind all his life could now see.

Remember what we talked about in Chapter 3. If people don't share their testimony of healing about what God has done, how will others hear?

When this woman heard those miracle testimonies, faith started rising in her heart. Yet even after hearing the testimonies, this woman still had to face her own "point of no return" — the moment when a radical thought entered her mind: *"Go find Jesus."*

The woman must have responded to that thought with every reason why she *shouldn't* go out in public to find Jesus: *They'll start screaming, "Unclean!"* — *or they might even stone me!*

But then that thought came again: *"Go find Jesus, and just touch the hem of His garment."* It was the quiet, delivering voice of the Holy Spirit helping her. He had the key this woman needed to unlock her answer: *"No matter what anyone else thinks, just do it."*

I can't even imagine the thoughts that the woman had to fight off to leave her house and make it through that crowd. She risked people rejecting and vilifying her — "Get away from me, you unclean woman!" She even risked being killed for violating the Law. She had no idea what she was going to face by going out in public. She was risking everything.

But this woman was following the hope that had been ignited in her heart: *"Go find Jesus, and just touch the hem of His robe."* That wasn't her original thought — any more than it was *my* original thought to turn on the radio that day at the very moment when the radio preacher was about to ask the question I needed to hear: "Do you really want to be healed?"

It wasn't the voice of God thundering from a mountain to this woman who was suffering with the blood disease; it was just the whisper of a thought that couldn't be ignored. But it *was* the delivering voice of God, and it got her moving toward her miracle: *I don't care what happens; I have to get to Jesus because I believe my answer is there. He healed the others, and He has the power to heal me too!*

…She came behind Him in the crowd and touched His garment. For she said, "If only I may touch His clothes, I shall be made well." Immediately the fountain of her blood was dried up, and she felt in her body that she was healed of the affliction.

Mark 5:27-29

It was just the whisper of a thought that couldn't be ignored. But it *was* the delivering voice of God, and it got her moving toward her miracle.

"…She *said*…'I shall be made well.'" This woman experienced the blessing of using her mouth to fulfill God's covenant on the earth through speech. And as her heart agreed with the words she was saying, *her* voice became the delivering voice of faith in that situation — the word sent from Heaven that changed *everything*.

THE KEY TO UNLOCK OUR DELIVERANCE

Possibly one of the most powerful instances of God's delivering voice is the quiet whisper within our own spirits as new creations. Jesus healed us physically when He redeemed us spiritually. He paid the total price. We simply need to agree with Him when He whispers, *"I've done everything needed; all that's left is to receive."*

When we hear the delivering voice of God, His words to us always contain a key that will unlock our answer — if we will only use it. We can't just stare at that key; we have to actually pick it up and *use* it to unlock our answer.

That's what I did when I heard that woman radio preacher ask, "Do you really want to be healed?" I immediately recognized it was the Holy Spirit speaking to me and revealing something in my heart that I needed to know. The key was a revelation from Heaven, and it had the power to unlock my healing. And my words — "Lord, I don't want any more attention because of this condition. I want to be healed!" — turned the key in the lock.

However, although I responded immediately to the delivering voice of God, nothing changed outwardly at that moment. Several weeks earlier, I'd heard that first radio preacher say that Jesus paid for my healing as well as for my salvation. For me, it was a brand-new revelation. Ever since, I'd been confessing the Word about my healing.

Weeks passed, and I still didn't see any difference, but I just kept doing what I knew to do. I just knew that hope had come alive in me to be healed, that I was no longer looking for attention through the sickness, and that I should keep speaking what the Word says about my healing.

During that "in-between" time, those close to me might have asked, "Why aren't you healed? You're believing God. You're confessing His Word. I hear you speak the Word all the time!" But they couldn't see into my heart. They couldn't see the faith- and miracle-producing Word of God that I was nurturing in my heart through the words I constantly spoke.

The words of my mouth were working in my heart and strengthening my faith, but I didn't know that. My understanding of the process was very limited. I was simply acting on what I had heard that first radio preacher say I needed to do — speak God's promises.

And don't you see Jesus' heart throughout my journey? He didn't get any joy out of the countless hours I had spent dealing with my face and the pain of that skin disease I'd endured over those 13 years. Actually, He was saying all along, *"I paid for that disease"* — and I finally "heard" Him. And then came the morning when I woke up, looked in the mirror, and discovered my face and neck had been healed and every sore had disappeared!

If you need healing in your body, here's something I want you to know, friend: It was *God's* idea for you to pick up this book and start pursuing your healing. It is absolutely His desire to heal you.

On the day I received that key to unlock my healing, it wasn't my idea to turn on the radio at that exact moment. I was being led by the Holy Spirit, and I didn't even know it! It was *His* idea for me to hear the question I needed to hear that day. The Holy Spirit was helping me get positioned to receive my healing — and He is doing the same for you.

> Weeks passed, and I still didn't see any difference, but I just kept doing what I knew to do. I just knew that hope had come alive in me to be healed, that I was no longer looking for attention through the sickness, and that I should keep speaking what the Word says about my healing.

HOLD FAST TILL YOUR HEALING MANIFESTS!

It takes the power of the Holy Spirit as the Revealer for any of us to know what's in our own heart. But even if there's something in our heart that's hindering the manifestation of our healing, we can count on the Lord to show it to us as we keep standing on His Word. Psalm 36:9 says, "...In Your light we see light."

So if it seems like you've been standing in faith for a long time without receiving the manifestation of your healing, don't ever let go of the truth that Jesus completely paid the price for every sickness and disease. God will always be faithful to His Word. Just keep your eyes on Him and your spiritual ears attuned to Him, and refuse to become distracted by what may be hindering the healing process. Walk in the light of His Word, and He will guide you on your healing journey. He will see you completely through to victory!

What Jesus went through on the Cross was to bring healing to us. Now it's our responsibility to lay hold of that truth so that it's not just words on a page. Instead, we can say with conviction, "These are words for *me*. This is for *my* life."

What Jesus went through on the Cross was to bring healing to us. Now it's our responsibility to lay hold of that truth so that it's not just words on a page. Instead, we can say with conviction, "These are words for *me*. This is for *my* life."

Never let go of the truth of Isaiah 53:

Surely He has borne our griefs and carried our sorrows; yet we esteemed Him stricken, smitten by God, and afflicted. But He was wounded for our transgressions, He was bruised for our iniquities; the chastisement for our peace was upon Him, and by His stripes we are healed....

He had done no violence, nor was any deceit in His mouth. Yet it pleased the Lord to bruise Him; He has put Him to grief. When You make His soul an offering for sin, He shall see His seed, He shall prolong His days, and the pleasure of the Lord shall prosper in His hand.

Isaiah 53:4,5,9,10

Surely Jesus has borne our griefs and our sicknesses. *Surely* He has carried our sorrows and our pain.

God goes to great lengths in these verses to assure us that He agreed to the sacrifice of His Son. It was all for you and me. The Father's decision was very intentional, with full understanding of the consequences to Jesus. It pleased the Father to bruise His Son because they were in full agreement with the plan to rescue mankind.

God put our sicknesses and our diseases on Jesus so we wouldn't have to suffer with them. Maybe you haven't yet seen that truth manifested in your own situation, and the enemy is trying to steal the revelation of that truth from you through discouragement. *But don't give up.*

Jesus paid too great a price to free us from sickness and disease in our bodies for us to stop short of standing in faith for our healing. If for some reason we haven't seen the manifestation of what we're believing for, we need to just rest in God's faithfulness to His Word, knowing that we're still growing in faith and understanding.

I urge you not to let go of this truth. In fact, I pray that you will open your heart and mind even further and receive more revelation as you read further in this book and keep searching the Scriptures on this subject of healing. The enemy may be trying to steal your health from you, but just keep pressing in harder to receive your healing in the name of Jesus!

Sometimes when people hear that it's God's will to heal them and that Jesus bore their sicknesses on the Cross, they answer, "Yes, but I've prayed and I've tried to believe for healing in my body, but nothing has changed."

But you can't *try* to believe, just like you can't *try* to bake a cake. It's a decision — *you are going to bake a cake!* In much the same way, it's your decision to believe that healing is yours *and you are going to receive it!*

———— ⚬✣⚬ ————

God put our sicknesses and our diseases on Jesus so we wouldn't have to suffer with them. Maybe you haven't yet seen that truth manifested in your own situation, and the enemy is trying to steal the revelation of that truth from you through discouragement. *But don't give up.*

———— ⚬✣⚬ ————

The Bible gives you help in believing. Romans 10:17 says, "So then faith comes by hearing, and hearing by the word of God." When you read the Word of God, you begin to hear the Holy Spirit speaking to you through the words you're reading as He plants faith in your heart.

Jesus is such a wonderful Savior and Healer, and as we've seen, He is the express image of the desire and will of the Father (*see* Hebrews 1:3). That's who He is. As we look in the gospels, we read over and over again how Jesus performed miracles, raised people from the dead, and healed all who came to Him. That was Jesus walking out the Father's will on the earth.

So just keep your eyes on the Healer. As you draw near to Jesus, you move toward your miracle. Listen to His voice above all others, for in His voice is deliverance. Hold fast to what He has already said about your healing in His Word. As your heart agrees with His promises and your mouth speaks what He has said, *your* voice becomes the delivering voice of God in your situation, and your faith will make you whole.

It is God's will that you are healed and made whole. You have His Word on it!

5

HOPE PUSHES THROUGH TO THE MIRACLE

You have to be strong in these last days. You can't give up on receiving your miracle. You may have to push through some obstacles before you will hold your answer in your hand or see it with your eyes.

The woman with the issue of blood understood this truth all too well (*see* Mark 5:25-34). We discussed in Chapter 4 the power that rested in her decision to respond to the delivering voice of hope in her heart. Remember, this woman had been bleeding for 12 years. It's difficult to imagine how horrible that must have been for this woman — how exhausted she must have felt, how greatly she must have suffered.

You may have to push through some obstacles before you will hold your answer in your hand or see it with your eyes.

Under the Jewish Law, a person with this kind of disease was a social outcast, rejected by everyone. Leviticus chapter 5 describes how someone with this woman's condition was viewed under the Law. She was considered "an unclean thing" under the category of "human uncleanness" (*see* Leviticus 5:2,3). If someone even touched a surface where she had been sitting or lying down, that person would also have become unclean. No one could hug this woman or even give her a loving touch, because anyone who did would have instantly become unclean as well.

So not only was this woman suffering physically, but she was suffering emotionally. Not even her family members could touch her during those 12 long years that she had suffered with this disease. It was as if she had a big sign hanging on her that shouted, "UNCLEAN!" It's difficult to imagine the rejection this woman dealt with every day of her life for all those years.

If you have ever been rejected because of a condition you had no control over, you know what I'm talking about. Maybe you felt rejected because of what you looked like. Maybe you didn't walk right; your arm didn't function right; or you couldn't hear well. Whatever the case, you may know what it's like to be rejected because of something completely outside your control.

But that isn't the love of Jesus. He doesn't reject anyone. Whoever comes to the Father in His name, He receives unconditionally.

Nevertheless, that was the situation this woman faced. She had worn the identity of "unclean" that religion had placed on her for 12 years. Then came the moment when she heard others speak about the miracles of Jesus — and the delivering voice of the Holy Spirit birthed hope in this woman's heart.

Now a certain woman had a flow of blood for twelve years, and had suffered many things from many physicians. She had spent all that she had and was no better, but rather grew worse. When she heard about Jesus, she came behind Him in the crowd and touched His garment. For she said, "If only I may touch His clothes, I shall be made well."

Mark 5:25-28

This woman had spent all her money over the years looking for a natural answer. Then she heard of Jesus. What did she hear about Him? We can imagine. She heard that the eyes of the blind and the ears of the deaf were opened under His ministry. She heard that someone who couldn't walk was now walking. She may have even heard that a demon had been cast out of someone's child and now the child was normal. And as she heard about the miracles, a new sense of hope was born in her heart. She decided that if she could just touch His garment, she would be healed.

It doesn't make natural sense to believe that you're going to be healed just by touching someone's clothes, but that was this woman's faith. Where did her faith come from? It came from what she had heard. *The woman heard about the miracles Jesus had performed for people, and hope arose in her heart.*

This woman had worn the identity of "unclean" that religion had placed on her for 12 years. Then came the moment when she heard others speak about the miracles of Jesus — and the delivering voice of the Holy Spirit birthed hope in this woman's heart.

THIS DESPERATE WOMAN'S PRESS OF FAITH

Hope had opened the door for the woman with the issue of blood to begin pushing through to her miracle.

This woman had been hearing about Jesus' miracles. Maybe she had just gotten back from the doctor and spent the last of her money, yet was still bleeding. She didn't feel any better, and she was exhausted.

But the woman had been hearing about Jesus, so she began to think to herself, *Jesus has so much power! Everyone He prays for is getting healed. I know that I'm unclean and I'm not supposed to go out of my house. But no matter what people think about me, I have to do it. I believe that Jesus has so much power in Him that if I can get through that crowd and just touch the hem of His garment, even just a tassel, I can be healed.*

> The woman didn't know it, but she had tapped into a spiritual law as she kept saying to herself what she believed. An inner courage began to rise as she told herself to get up, walk out of the house, and go find Jesus.

The woman didn't know it, but she had tapped into a spiritual law as she kept saying to herself what she believed. An inner courage began to rise as she told herself to get up, walk out of the house, and go find Jesus.

The journey must have been challenging. The woman was still dealing with an issue of blood as she walked the distance to reach Jesus. But those thoughts that fueled her hope kept her pressing on as she drew near the crowd: *I don't know how I'm going to get to*

Jesus, but I'm going to somehow find a way. I don't have to touch Him. If I can just touch His garment, I'll be healed.

The woman wasn't asking Jesus to lay hands on her; she knew that she was unclean. She just wanted to grab a miracle in secret because a seed of faith had been planted in her heart: *I know if I can just touch Jesus' garment, I'm going to be healed!*

I can just imagine the scene when the woman was within a few yards of Jesus. She could hear His voice. Scholars say that the woman may have actually crawled on the ground in order to slip through the crushing crowd without anyone noticing. Her entire focus was just to get within arm's length of Jesus so she could secretly reach out and grab her healing.

It is the only place in the gospels I know of that someone came from behind Jesus to touch Him; everyone else came to speak to Him face to face. But this woman was unclean; she wasn't supposed to touch Him or anyone else.

Inching closer and closer to Jesus, the woman finally got near enough to stretch out her hand and touch the hem of His garment.

Immediately the fountain of her blood was dried up, and she felt in her body that she was healed of the affliction. And Jesus, immediately knowing in Himself that power had gone out of Him, turned around in the crowd and said, "Who touched My clothes?"

Mark 5:29,30

Immediately the blood stopped flowing and the woman's hemorrhaging ceased. Immediately Jesus was aware that the power of God had gone out of Him.

It had happened according to the woman's faith. Her faith had pulled healing power out of Jesus and into her body, and she knew that she was healed.

Jesus looked around and asked, "Who touched My clothes?" All kinds of people were jostling and pressing against Jesus — but He knew that someone had touched Him with the touch of faith.

Look at His disciples' response in verse 31:

But His disciples said to Him, "You see the multitude thronging You, and You say, 'Who touched Me?'"

The disciples didn't understand what had just happened. But Jesus didn't pay attention to what the disciples said; He *knew* that the power of God had gone out of Him. "And He looked around to see her who had done this thing" (v. 32). So we can see that the word of knowledge was working in Jesus at this moment, because He knew it was a woman who had touched Him.

You can just imagine. Everyone was focused on Jesus. After all, He was the reason they had all gathered. So when He stopped and looked around, they must have thought, *Why did Jesus stop? Why is He looking around?*

The woman also saw Jesus looking around to see who had touched Him. She heard Him ask, "Who touched Me?" She might have gasped as she realized, *He knows!*

Suddenly the woman's secret miracle wasn't so secret anymore, and fear must have risen up and threatened to take over in her mind. She knew that she was the one He was looking for, but she was so afraid. The Bible even says that she was trembling. But the secret was out. It was time for her to tell Jesus the whole truth.

Certainly this woman had to push through her fear to even draw attention to herself by answering Jesus — but the Bible says that is what she did. This woman spoke up and told Jesus the whole truth.

But the woman, fearing and trembling, knowing what had happened to her, came and fell down before Him and told Him the whole truth.

Mark 5:33

Can you imagine? The woman probably said something like, "I'm the one who touched You, Jesus. And I'm not bleeding anymore — I'm healed! I'll tell You how it happened.

"I had been bleeding for 12 years. It's been so horrible. You know, Jesus, that anyone in that condition is declared unclean. All these years, I haven't touched my children, my husband, or my friends. I've just stayed in my house — lonely, rejected, and unclean.

"Then I started hearing about You, Jesus. I heard that You open the eyes of the blind. I heard that the lame start walking after You pray for them. I heard that You pray for the demon-possessed and they get set free! And I also heard that You fed all those people on a mountain with just two fish and five loaves!

"After hearing all that, I said to myself, *I believe if I can just touch the hem of Jesus' garment, I'll be healed.* So I did what I had to do to get here, Jesus. It was a struggle, but the entire way, I just kept saying to myself, *All I need to do is touch the hem of His garment, and I'll be healed.*

"When I got here, I got down on my knees and started crawling through the crowd. Then I saw Your feet and the hem of Your garment, and I just reached out and touched the hem for a split second. And when I did, this issue of blood that has afflicted my body for 12 years *stopped* — and I'm healed!"

'GO IN PEACE'

I love how Jesus replied so simply to the woman:

And He said to her, "Daughter, your faith has made you well. Go in peace, and be healed of your affliction."

Mark 5:34

"Go in peace," Jesus said to the woman. He knew all about that sickness that this woman had carried and how it had stolen her peace. And He didn't chastise her for violating the Law by coming out in public to find Him. In fact, Jesus commended the woman for having the courage to act on her faith, and He pointed to that faith as the reason she was made whole.

Consider this: A Jewish ruler named Jairus had approached Jesus right before this woman reached Him (*see* Mark 5:22,23). Jairus was a very powerful man; this woman was an outcast of society, a rejected person no one wanted to be around.

The woman with the issue of blood didn't walk up to Jesus the way Jairus did; she came from behind. In Jairus' case, it was he who stopped Jesus to talk to Him. But in the case of this woman, it was her *faith* that stopped Jesus and caused the healing virtue to flow out of the Master and into her, instantly bringing wholeness to her body.

Right now is *your* opportunity for your faith to get Jesus' attention. It's not because you've done everything right. He's simply inviting you into His healing presence.

It was Jesus who said, "Come to Me, all you who labor and are heavy laden, and I will give you rest" (Matthew 11:28). It was Jesus who said, "I am not a High Priest you can't touch. I've been tempted in every way that you've been tempted. I didn't sin, but I understand" (*see* Hebrews 4:15).

And in Mark 5:34, Jesus spoke these words to this woman: "...Daughter, your faith has made you well. Go in peace, and be healed of your affliction."

Right now is *your* opportunity for your faith to get Jesus' attention. It's not because you've done everything right. He's simply inviting you into His healing presence.

Jesus didn't rebuke her. He didn't say indignantly, "You touched Me, and you were unclean!" He didn't say, "Why did you come? You risked making others unclean in order to get to Me!"

No, instead, Jesus called this woman "Daughter" and simply told her to go in peace to live her life healed and whole.

HEALED IN THE NIGHT

I've always compared myself to this woman with the issue of blood. I talked to you in the last two chapters about that terrible skin disease on my face and neck I suffered with for 13 years. Then the day came when I turned on the radio and heard for the first time that by Jesus' stripes, I was healed.

I don't know how it's possible that I hadn't heard that before in all my Christian life. But I heard it that day, and, as I shared previously with you, such an amazing thing happened in my heart. The radio preacher's words that day became the delivering voice of God, breaking into my world of despair.

For the woman with the issue of blood, hope arose in her heart and stirred her to take action by faith — and the same thing happened to me. As I listened to the radio preacher's message that day, hope came into my heart!

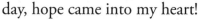

> For the woman with the issue of blood, hope arose in her heart and stirred her to take action by faith — and the same thing happened to me. As I listened to the radio preacher's message that day, hope came into my heart!

I asked the Lord, "Do You mean that *I* can be healed?" You see, it became very personal. It wasn't "I know You can heal all those other people." It was "God, You would heal *me*?"

First Corinthians 13:13 says: "And now abide faith, hope, love, these three; but the greatest of these is love." We talk a lot about how love is the greatest of these — but what about faith and hope? Hope is powerful. And I'm telling you, when hope came to my heart, that is what opened the door for me to receive my healing.

I began to believe God's Word and confess every day that by Jesus' stripes, I was healed. *In hope, I was pushing through to my miracle!*

Every morning I'd look in the mirror and see the disease on my face, unchanged — and then I'd say or I'd sing, "By His stripes

I am healed!" I didn't see any change, but I just kept confessing that every day.

Then came the day when I was in my car, and I heard another radio preacher ask, "Do you really want to be healed?" — and the Holy Spirit revealed to me that a part of my soul had taken hold of this disease because it gave me pity and attention from my mother. And as I shared earlier, the moment that revelation came to me, I said, "Jesus, I repent. I don't want anyone's attention. I want to be healed!"

Another month or so went by. I still looked the same, and I was still confessing the Word of God every day. I was holding fast to the hope that had come alive in my heart when I realized I could be healed.

Then one night I went to bed just as I had every other night for 13 years, with the evidence of that disease all over my face and neck: the pain, the bruising, the sores. I didn't know that this wasn't going to be a normal night — that this was going to be my miracle night!

The next morning when I looked in the mirror, *my face and my neck were absolutely clear.* My face, swollen with the poison of the skin disease just hours earlier, looked so different that people thought I had lost ten pounds!

Friend, I don't know when Jesus did it. I don't know if He took 1 second, 20 minutes, or the entire 8 hours of sleep. All I know is that Jesus touched my face and eradicated that disease! *He healed me in the night.*

THE HEALER GIVES US OUR LIFE BACK

When Jesus spoke the words, "Go in peace," that meant the woman was completely healed — not only in her body, but in her mind and her emotions. Her life had been stolen from her for 12 years, but in a split second, she was given her life back.

That's what healing does. *For those who are healed by the power of God, He gives them their life back.* What a beautiful demonstration of God's love for people is contained in that one statement!

When Jesus healed me, I never had to go to another doctor for that ailment. I never had another blemish — *ever*. I was never embarrassed because of my face ever again. I was never turned down from another job. My face and neck were never in pain again. My face never again looked swollen and bruised. *When Jesus gave me my healing, He gave me my life back.*

Jesus is the same yesterday, today, and forever (*see* Hebrews 13:8). He gave us His Holy Spirit, and the Holy Spirit is just like Jesus (*see* John 14:16-18). The Holy Spirit's power is there with you right now as you read these words. I have experienced Jesus the Healer. This woman with the issue of blood experienced Jesus the Healer. And it's God's will for *you* to experience Him as Jesus the Healer!

Jesus is in the business of healing us and giving our lives back to us. Sickness is a thief — but Jesus is the Restorer.

If you're sick or have pain in your body right now, you know what I'm talking about. Sickness can steal your peace and rob you of your joy. Jesus knew that had been the case for this woman, so He said to her, *"Go in peace."*

Jesus wants you to walk in peace. He wants to reveal Himself to you as your Healer of every pain, sickness, and disease. His presence is there upon you right now.

You might be saying to yourself, *But I don't read my Bible enough; I don't pray enough. I haven't even been tithing.*

Jesus is in the business of healing us and giving our lives back to us. Sickness is a thief — but Jesus is the Restorer.

None of those things is the determining factor. Jesus is inviting you to receive the healing He has already purchased for you.

That's why it was on my heart to write this book. I want to tell you that it's not just about the healing power — it's about *the Person* who *has* the healing power! It's about you getting to know Jesus. It's about loving Him and knowing that He loves you. It's about being touched by His presence and His power so that you, too, can *go in peace* into the days ahead and enjoy the life that He gives back to you as He makes you healed and whole!

YOUR FAITH IS ALL YOU NEED

Jesus so desires for us to walk in divine health that He has provided many ways for us to receive healing. For instance:

- Mark 16:18 says that believers can lay hands on the sick and they will be healed.

- James 5:14,15 says that the elders of the church can come and anoint the sick with oil, and the sick will be healed.

- Matthew 18:19 says that we can pray the prayer of agreement and receive the healing we ask for and agree upon.

- Mark 11:23,24 says that by the words we say and the faith in our hearts, we can be healed.

Jesus conquered sickness and disease on the Cross with His own blood. He made sure we would have many ways to experience His healing power.

This woman with the issue of blood received healing because of the faith she had in her heart. Jesus confirmed this when He said to her, "Daughter, go in peace; your faith has made you well."

It could be that you, like this woman, have no other way to receive your healing but the way of your own faith. But your faith is all that you need! However, it can't be a passive, "Let's wait and see what God does," kind of faith. You may have to use your faith to *push through* to your miracle.

It's very obvious that this woman was *involved* with her faith. She was speaking; she was pushing through that crowd full of people who were probably talking about her — "Who is this? How dare she come here?"

Friend, we know that Jesus is the only One who can give to us the mighty, wonderful things He has for us in these last days. If we're going to receive those blessings, we will have to maintain the attitude that we don't care about what others think of us.

This is so important. Can't you see that quality in this woman? She could have said, "There are just too many people out there where Jesus is. I can't go to Him — they'll all curse me. They might even hit me. I just can't do it!"

But the woman cared more about receiving what Jesus could give her than what other people thought. She said, "If I can just touch the hem of His garment, *I will be healed.*"

For us to receive our healing that Jesus already purchased by His blood, we're going to have to do what He has told us to do. We'll have to establish it in our hearts that regardless of what other people say, we will be bold to believe for our healing and forgive those who hurt us. We will have to make the decision, *No matter what, I'm going to do what God has put in my heart.*

That's what this woman did. She said, "I don't care what people say. Even if they start screaming, "Unclean!" I'm going to push through that crowd, and I am going to receive my healing!"

I'm thinking of a woman I know who has that kind of attitude. She has endured a mighty struggle with a certain sickness. She has endured a lot of pain; she's had a lot of sleepless nights.

> The woman cared more about receiving what Jesus could give her than what other people thought. She said, "If I can just touch the hem of His garment, *I will be healed.*"

There were a couple of times when she almost died. But this dear woman of God has the tenacity of a bulldog, and she will *not* let go of His healing power!

The woman says with all confidence, "I am going to be healed!" And little by little, she is receiving her health. Little by little, this symptom and that symptom are going away.

This woman is not letting go; she doesn't listen to the opinions of others. She says, "I know what I want; I know what I've heard, and I'm going to receive my healing!" She's just like that woman with the issue of blood. She is determined to press forward despite the difficulties and to grab 100 percent of the healing that is hers through what Jesus purchased for her on the Cross. And she is absolutely going to be 100-percent healed in her body because she is refusing to give up!

This kind of fight of faith requires true tenacity. Some Christians get discouraged and give up after confessing the Word and making declarations for a week without receiving the healing they desire. But those who develop a "never-give-up" tenacity and keep pressing on are the ones who ultimately receive their miracle.

PULLING DOWN SYSTEMS OF THOUGHT THAT HINDER HEALING

Why are some able to achieve that level of tenacity in their faith while others get discouraged and give up? For one thing, there may be systems of thinking that people have been stuck in for years, set up like roadblocks on their path to healing. For instance, someone might think, *I'm not worthy to receive Jesus' provision of healing.* Or maybe a person is stuck in the thought: *Well, my dad, my uncle, and my aunt all died of that disease, so I'll probably die of it too.*

> There may be systems of thinking that people have been stuck in for years, set up like roadblocks on their path to healing.

But those kinds of thoughts originate from the enemy! They are part of a system of wrong thinking that we have to deliberately pull down. That requires an intentional focus on what God says in His Word.

God isn't holding back your miracle, but there may be a system of thinking in your mind that doesn't agree with simply receiving that miracle by faith. For instance, fear may be trying to overtake your emotions, causing you to focus on the worst-case scenario. But just like the woman with the issue of blood, you have to push through that fear and keep moving toward your miracle. Just like that woman, you have to decide you want to touch Jesus more than you want to pay attention to fear!

I've been in that place in my life. I've said to the Lord, "Jesus, I'm grabbing hold of You harder than this fear is grabbing hold of me!" And do you know what happened when I did that? My situation started changing. The shift began the minute I said, "I rebuke this fear! I reject it, and I'm taking Your hand, Lord. I'm moving forward!"

These verses in particular helped me pull down the stronghold of fear in my life as I meditated on their truth and declared them with my mouth:

> **"Fear not, for I am with you; be not dismayed, for I am your God. I will strengthen you, Yes, I will help you, I will uphold you with My righteous right hand…. For I, the Lord your**

I've said to the Lord, "Jesus, I'm grabbing hold of You harder than this fear is grabbing hold of me!" And do you know what happened when I did that? My situation started changing.

God, will hold your right hand, saying to you, 'Fear not, I will help you.'"

Isaiah 41:10,13

For God has not given us a spirit of fear, but of power and of love and of a sound mind.

2 Timothy 1:7

Friend, when you refuse to give up and you keep pulling down every thought that has kept you from believing, you are pushing through to your miracle just like that woman with the issue of blood did. I promise you — if you don't give up and you continue to agree with what Jesus did for you, you *will* push through to your miracle!

6

~

WHEN GOD'S MERCY
MEETS FAITH

It's true that people are able to receive their healing as they push through every obstacle and stand firm in their faith in Jesus as their Healer. But God is bigger than a person's faith. He is merciful; He loves this world.

For God so loved the world that He gave His only begotten Son, that whoever believes in Him should not perish but have everlasting life.

John 3:16

Throughout the Church Age and in these present times, there have been men and women who cursed God's name, yet God came to them in His mercy to heal them and set them free. It wasn't their faith that activated their miracle; it was a manifestation of His mercy.

We serve a merciful God. I know of testimonies of people who have been healed when they weren't even believing to get healed at all. In one situation, a minister was holding meetings and ministering in the power of God, and several people decided to attend the meeting for the sole purpose of criticizing him. But while the group stood there criticizing, the Holy Spirit touched their bodies and healed them!

Yet at the same time, I never want to diminish the role of faith in our lives. Hebrews 11:6 tells us that it is impossible to please God without faith and that we who come to Him must believe He is a rewarder of those who diligently seek Him. We need to use our faith.

Never stop pursuing faith, but always leave room for God's mercy. And if you have the opportunity to lay hands on an unsaved person and pray for that person's healing, you should absolutely do that. Miracles draw unbelievers to God, so get your hands out of your pockets and lay them on the unbelieving. Let them see how great our God is!

THE POWER OF FAITH
THAT WON'T TAKE NO FOR AN ANSWER

I want to show you a powerful example of God's mercy and compassion in action. When a Gentile woman came to Jesus with a desperate plea for help, she had faith that wouldn't take no for an answer.

> **Then Jesus went out from there and departed to the region of Tyre and Sidon. And behold, a woman of Canaan came from that region and cried out to Him, saying, "Have mercy on me, O Lord, Son of David! My daughter is severely demon-possessed." But He answered her not a word.**
>
> **And His disciples came and urged Him, saying, "Send her away, for she cries out after us." But He answered and said, "I was not sent except to the lost sheep of the house of Israel."**

Then she came and worshiped Him, saying, "Lord, help me!" But He answered and said, "It is not good to take the children's bread and throw it to the little dogs." And she said, "Yes, Lord, yet even the little dogs eat the crumbs which fall from their masters' table."

Then Jesus answered and said to her, "O woman, great is your faith! Let it be to you as you desire." And her daughter was healed from that very hour.

Matthew 15:21-28

This Canaanite woman was a Gentile, not a Hebrew, but she was crying out to Jesus for help. That was actually an amazing act of courage for this woman because she knew that she was a Canaanite woman and that Jesus was a Jew — and she knew that Jews and Canaanites didn't get along. But the Canaanite woman didn't let that stop her, because she had evidently heard of the miracles Jesus was performing wherever He went and she believed He could help her demon-possessed daughter.

I don't know another place in Scripture where someone is referred to as *severely* demon-possessed. But that's how this woman described her daughter.

Can you even imagine how this Canaanite woman felt? Maybe you've had a troubled child or a spouse on drugs or someone in your family addicted to alcohol, and you've felt the unrelenting pressure of that situation. Perhaps you've had the thought, *I need help to get out of this!* The constant chaos of that kind of stress can wear on you and sap your energy, and sometimes it can even steal your health.

So here was this Gentile mother who intensely loved her daughter, yet she had watched her daughter suffer *severely*. We know from other instances in the Bible how demon possession manifested at times — with afflicted individuals foaming at the mouth, going into convulsions, throwing themselves into fire or water, cutting themselves, or screaming (*see* Mark 5:5; 9:14-22). I cannot even fathom what it was like for this mother to see the child she loved in so much suffering. It's not difficult to imagine the burden, stress, heartache, and pain that this would cause any parent.

This mother came to Jesus *desperate* to find a way to help her afflicted daughter. And from the moment the woman began to cry out to Jesus about the nature of her problem, He was already having mercy on her; she just didn't know it yet. Jesus didn't stand back like a judge and say, "Of course you have a problem. Look at who you are — a Gentile woman." No, He simply didn't say anything at that point.

The woman may have thought, *This is NOT what I was hoping for — that Jesus wouldn't even answer me, and here I am crying out to Him.*

But Jesus' silence doesn't always mean no, and His timing is perfect.

Of course, Jesus' response of silence presented a different kind of challenge for this Canaanite woman, and she had to make a decision in the moment about how she was going to respond. The woman could have gotten discouraged right then and walked away. She could have viewed Jesus' silence to her plea for help as just another instance in her life of being rejected.

> Jesus' silence doesn't always mean no, and His timing is perfect.

Then in verse 23, the disciples, who were obviously irritated by the woman, came to Jesus and urged Him, "…Send her away, for she cries out after us." Only then did Jesus finally speak, saying, "…I was not sent except to the lost sheep of the house of Israel."

At that point, the Canaanite woman was faced with an even greater temptation to just give up and leave, because being denied help is worse than being ignored. If we had faced a similar situation, by this time, most of us would have thought, *First Jesus ignored me; then the disciples told Him to make me go away; and now Jesus says He was sent only to help the house of Israel. It looks like I'm not going to receive the help I'm asking for. Maybe all I heard about Jesus is true, but I don't think it's going to be true for me.*

But that was *not* this Canaanite woman's response. She still had hope in her heart that Jesus was going to heal and deliver her daughter.

Maybe you have expectant hope in your heart that you're going to receive the healing miracle you need for yourself or for a loved one. Don't give up on that hope in Jesus' healing power and His bountiful mercy. Follow this woman's example — stand firm in your faith in His power and His willingness to heal, and keep pushing through to your miracle!

'LORD, HELP ME!'

This Canaanite woman could have just complied with what the disciples wanted and left feeling disappointed, and her daughter would have remained severely demon-possessed. But verse 25 reveals the woman's response to Jesus' words: "Then she came and worshiped him, saying, 'Lord, help me!'"

The woman lowered herself prostrate to the floor and began worshiping Jesus at His feet.

"Lord, help me."

It wasn't a religious prayer. The woman just said those three simple words — a brief prayer that was humble, respectful, hopeful, and desperate.

God isn't looking for long prayers from us; He's just looking for a heart connection with someone who says, "Lord, I'm desperate. I don't have anywhere else to turn for an answer, and I'm looking to You. Please help me."

I can't tell you how many people have a testimony like this to share. People come to a place where they don't have any other options for help. They get desperate and say, "I don't really know who You are, God, but if You're there, I ask You to help me." And after they pray, God intervenes and help comes! That person gets saved, healed, and delivered!

The key is this: the humble turning of a person's heart toward Jesus from a place of desperation to receive help from Him. That's where this woman was; she was desperate and she put her hope in Jesus. And she cried out with a very simple prayer: "Lord, help me!"

> God isn't looking for long prayers from us; He's just looking for a heart connection with someone who says, "Lord, I'm desperate. I don't have anywhere else to turn for an answer, and I'm looking to You. Please help me."

THE POWER OF HUMILITY IN BELIEVING

Then Jesus spoke to the woman again. This time He said, "...It is not good to take the children's bread and throw it to the little dogs" (v. 26).

At that point, the Canaanite woman could have become discouraged and felt rejected. After all, the Son of God had just likened her to a dog! Jesus' words made it clear that the children of the Covenant have access to this bread, but that this woman was outside the Covenant. Yet look at how she responded: "...Yes, Lord, yet even the little dogs eat the crumbs which fall from their masters' table" (v. 27).

So the woman was saying, "Okay, I accept that. I agree with that. I know that I'm not worthy according to the Law of the children of Israel. But I don't have to have the whole loaf. Just give me a little crumb that falls from the master's table. I'll be thankful for a crumb!"

What humility and faith this Canaanite woman displayed in her response to Jesus! Her daughter wasn't even present in the room, but the desperate mother was ready to receive the girl's deliverance by faith at Jesus' word. She said to Jesus, "Just give me one of the crumbs when it falls from the children's bread of healing. All I need is a little crumb." This Gentile woman understood that there is as much healing power in the crumbs as there is in the loaf of bread, because God is the Source of healing for all.

PARTAKING OF THE BREAD PROVIDED FOR US

The woman's response revealed what she believed about Jesus, and it is the response of faith that He is always listening for. Jesus replied, "...O woman, great is your faith! Let it be to you as you desire..." (v. 28). And the girl was healed and delivered that very hour as a result of her mother's faith.

Isn't that amazing? One word from Jesus is all the woman needed and all she desired to hear. But she didn't hear that word immediately. She asked and asked again; she was seemingly rejected several times. But she just kept asking until she received that one word from Jesus that she was desperate to hear: "Let it be to you as you desire."

That's the word we want to hear from Jesus as well: *"Let it be as you desire."* But sometimes we give up too quickly. We think, *Well, I've been asking for two weeks for my healing, and I'm not healed yet. I've been asking God for the finances I need for two months, but the money hasn't come.* And then we stop pushing through to our miracle.

But not this woman. She was "rejected" over and over again, but she kept pressing in. She was saying, in effect, "I know that I might be seen as a dog in this culture, but even the dogs are given the crumbs. Please, Lord, help me. You can give the whole loaf to Your children. Just give me a crumb, and it will be enough to heal and deliver my daughter."

The woman's simple faith touched Jesus so much that He said, "Your faith is great! You can have what you desire." And her daughter was healed in that same hour.

I love the moment when the person who so desperately needs a miracle suddenly receives that miracle. That's what happened to me the night I went to bed still in my seemingly unhealed condition, having suffered 13 years from that skin disease, and I woke up the next morning with no disease.

That's what happens when someone who received a diagnosis of cancer hears the doctor's dire prognosis but decides to trust God. And then a day comes when the doctor says, "I don't know where the cancer went — there is no trace of cancer in you!" A believer who experiences that moment didn't receive just a crumb — he received the whole loaf that is provided for God's children!

Oh, that we would take hold of all that God has given us! Jesus said that He *is* the Bread of Heaven (*see* John 6:51). Jesus is God, who came to earth in the flesh, and He said, "Take of Me. I fed My children manna in the wilderness, but now I'm feeding you with Living Bread that is never going to pass away, because it represents My very self."

In that divine loaf is your financial provision, your healing, and your deliverance from oppression, from depression, from drug addiction, from family turmoil — from any and every bondage that comes from the kingdom of darkness. God has laid out His life through the Person of Jesus Christ, and He offers to you and me *the whole loaf*!

Jesus is God, who came to earth in the flesh, and He said, "Take of Me. I fed My children manna in the wilderness, but now I'm feeding you with Living Bread that is never going to pass away, because it represents My very self."

THE POWER IN ONE 'CRUMB'

It will help us to consider how this woman could have chosen to respond differently. When Jesus said, "I was sent to the house of Israel," and then went on to say, "This bread is only for the children of Israel," she could have gotten discouraged and walked away. And if she had done that, her daughter would have continued to be tormented by demons. But this Canaanite woman chose to push through feelings of rejection and unworthiness to receive her miracle.

During the first Communion that Jesus shared with His disciples, He likened His broken body to bread. Then Jesus told the disciples to eat the bread in remembrance of Him (*see* Matthew 26:26).

Sometimes we, like this woman, don't feel worthy to partake of the whole loaf of bread that Jesus provided through the stripes He endured. For those of us who are His children, that feeling is truly a lie of the enemy that Satan tries to feed us, because the truth is that Jesus has freely invited us as God's children to sit at His table and freely partake of every blessing offered — including the bread of healing.

Yet even this woman who didn't belong to the house of God understood that she could receive deliverance and healing for her daughter from just a tiny crumb of that divine loaf. The girl could be delivered and healed according to her mother's faith and because of God's mercy toward her.

It is absolutely God's will for every one of us to eat of this bread — to partake of His power, His life, His goodness. Even if it's a crumb, it all comes from the same loaf, and in that bread is healing.

That Canaanite woman wasn't of the house of Israel, yet her demon-possessed daughter was healed and delivered that very hour because the woman believed.

What does God want to give to you right now? What do you need from Him? Do you need a miracle in your body? Does a loved one need to be healed or delivered?

Jesus has invited us to the table. The children's bread is there, ready to be partaken of — and even the crumbs have enough power to heal and deliver to the uttermost.

HEALING FOR *ALL* — HEALING FOR *YOU*

I just want you to get a glimpse of what that whole loaf looks like. We see it in the next verses that tell us what happened after Jesus delivered that young Canaanite girl from being severely demon-possessed.

Jesus departed from there, skirted the Sea of Galilee, and went up on the mountain and sat down there. Then great multitudes came to Him, having with them the lame, blind, mute, maimed, and many others; and they laid them down at Jesus' feet, and He healed them.

Matthew 15:29,30

That's what is in the loaf: healing of *all* who came to Jesus. The lame, the blind, the maimed — all who were oppressed of the devil — found healing and deliverance when they partook of that divine loaf.

Are you struggling with pain or other symptoms in your body? Are you feeling oppressed in your mind and emotions? Whatever you're dealing with, this loaf is for you. Healing is for you right now. Just agree with the Holy Spirit and reach out to take what is yours!

Jesus has invited us to the table. The children's bread is there, ready to be partaken of — and even the crumbs have enough power to heal and deliver to the uttermost.

Talk to the Father. Tell Him, "You know what I need before I even say it, Father. I need healing; I need deliverance in my mind and emotions. My family members need deliverance. Lord, I'm asking You to help me. I believe that what Jesus did on the Cross was for me, and I partake of His power and provision right now in Jesus' Name."

Tell the Holy Spirit, "I know I've struggled with fear and doubt, Holy Spirit, but I also know that You have compassion on me. So I'm agreeing with You right now that Jesus is the Bread of Heaven and He gave His life so I could partake of the miracle I need. In this loaf is my healing, my deliverance, my financial provision, and help in my relationships. I take hold right now of Your power, Holy Spirit, and I won't stop pressing in for my miracle until I see my answer with my own eyes!"

If you prayed that prayer, you can know that God is moving in your life, because He's not a liar and His presence is right there with you as you read these words. You can reach out by faith and take whatever you need, knowing that Jesus wants to give it to you. He's not standing there holding that divine loaf, ready to pull it away from you when you reach for it. No! Jesus said in John 6:51, "I am the living bread which came down from heaven. If anyone eats of this bread, he will live forever; and the bread that I shall give is My flesh, which I shall give for the life of the world."

The Bible says Jesus didn't come to condemn but to *save* the world (*see* John 3:17). He came to earth so that He could give Himself to you. He is freely offering Himself, His great healing power, and His mercy and compassion to you right now. You simply have to receive it by faith.

7

SEIZE YOUR MOMENT!

The woman with the issue of blood and the Canaanite woman had a very crucial thing in common: *They took advantage of a Heaven-appointed moment.* They each kept pursuing their miracle and pushing through all obstacles until they received the healing or deliverance that their heart desired.

In Chapter 4, we also looked briefly at the case of blind Bartimaeus. Bartimaeus was another one who, desperate to receive his healing, *took hold* of his moment as Jesus walked by.

> **Now they came to Jericho. As He [Jesus] went out of Jericho with His disciples and a great multitude, blind Bartimaeus, the son of Timaeus, sat by the road begging. And when he heard that it was Jesus of Nazareth, he began to cry out and say, "Jesus, Son of David, have mercy on me!" Then many warned him to be quiet; but he cried out all the more, "Son of David, have mercy on me!"**
>
> **Mark 10:46-48**

Bartimaeus had been blind all his life. As he got up that morning and went about his normal routine, putting on his garment that identified him as a blind beggar with the right to beg,

Bartimaeus wasn't thinking, *This is going to be my miracle day.* But that's exactly what it was going to be!

RECOGNIZE THE MOMENT OF OPPORTUNITY

There blind Bartimaeus sat in his customary spot, begging as usual. Then came the moment when he heard that Jesus of Nazareth was walking by. He couldn't see what was happening; he was completely dependent on his sense of hearing. But Bartimaeus immediately began to cry out. He knew: *This is my opportunity!*

Then certain people, filled with their own opinions, started telling Bartimaeus to be quiet: "Oh, blind Bartimaeus, hush! I've known you all my life. You're blind, and you're a beggar. That's who you are, and that's who you'll always be."

These men and women were pouring out their negative opinions about blind Bartimaeus on his appointed miracle day. They were telling him, "Blind Bartimaeus, you've been blind all your life. Just be quiet. You're bothering Jesus. He's not going to pay attention to you. Who do you think you are? You've always been that way, and you're going to stay that way." But blind Bartimaeus didn't let those opinions stop him — he just kept crying out!

Sometimes those negative opinions come from ourselves: *Well, I've had this physical issue for so long. I guess I'll be this way the rest of my life. I'll just watch everyone else get their miracle.*

But that wasn't blind Bartimaeus. He wasn't going to listen to the naysayers. *Nothing* was going to stop him from crying out.

We can take courage from this man's example. The people told him to shut up, and he just cried out all the louder! And he didn't just cry out once. Over and over, Bartimaeus yelled, "Son of David, have mercy on me. Have mercy on me! I don't see You; I don't know where You are — but I know You're close! Son of David, have mercy on me!"

Bartimaeus was taking hold of his moment! He had an attitude that refused to be deterred from pursuing his miracle of healing. That is exactly the kind of attitude that the Church needs to adopt — that when the world tells us to shut up, we cry out in faith even louder! We have to let people see this great God on the inside of us and refuse to let *anyone* intimidate us or deprive us of our miracle!

Verse 49 reveals Jesus' response to Bartimaeus' persistence in pursuing the miracle of healing that he so desired:

> **So Jesus stood still and commanded him to be called. Then they called the blind man, saying to him, "Be of good cheer. Rise, He is calling you."**

That's how fickle people can be with their negative opinions. Far too often we give up our conviction that propels us to pursue our miracle because of the negative opinions of people — people who are liable to change their opinion in the next moment!

Bartimaeus was taking hold of his moment! He had an attitude that refused to be deterred from pursuing his miracle of healing. That is exactly the kind of attitude that the Church needs to adopt — that when the world tells us to shut up, we cry out in faith even louder!

The very people who had been so rude to blind Bartimaeus changed their tune as soon as Jesus stopped and beckoned the blind man to come to Him. They started saying, "Oh, be of good cheer. Rise and come — He's calling you. Just forget the fact that five minutes ago I told you to shut up and that you weren't worthy. You can be of good cheer now."

This is how people can be at times, so we have to decide what song *we're* going to sing no matter what. We know that blind Bartimaeus tuned in to only one song that day — the song of faith. He said, "Jesus is going to have mercy on me and heal me today — *period.*"

And throwing aside his garment, he rose and came to Jesus.

Mark 10:50

What was in that garment? Bartimaeus' entire identity — his lunch ticket, his profession. Everything that blind Bartimaeus' life was built on was in that garment. Jesus knew what that garment stood for, and He took note that Bartimaeus walked up to Him without it.

And throwing aside his garment, he rose and came to Jesus. So Jesus answered and said to him, "What do you want Me to do for you?" The blind man said to Him, "Rabboni, that I may receive my sight."

Mark 10:50,51

I used to think that was such a strange question for Jesus to ask Bartimaeus, because the answer seemed obvious. But blind Bartimaeus needed to say what he desired from Jesus, because his life up to that moment seemed to have his destiny sealed. Even the crowd around Bartimaeus told him that he couldn't have his sight and progress from the place he had been all those years.

Yet despite all the obstacles blind Bartimaeus faced, he hadn't given up, and now he was standing before the Healer Himself. The moment of his lifetime had arrived.

Bartimaeus couldn't see Jesus standing there in front of him, but he could hear His voice.

Then Jesus said to him, "Go your way; your *faith* has made you well." And immediately he received his sight and followed Jesus on the road.

Mark 10:52

I believe that at times we have missed some "immediatelies" because we listened to the opinions of others. Someone may have said to us, "You're ridiculous for believing for a miracle in your body." And as a result, we gave up on our miracle — because of what someone else said.

But there is a reward for staying in faith: We stay positioned for the moment of our miracle.

You know, the place of our problem — whether it's sickness or disease, a physical disability, or a mental or emotional issue — is a real place, and the temptation is to focus on that place and examine it all the time. But the miracle that is waiting for us is a real place too. And that miracle has already been bought and paid for by Jesus' precious blood!

Blind Bartimaeus was absolutely a blind beggar. That was his whole identity. But then this man seized his moment and pursued

There is a reward for staying in faith: We stay positioned for the moment of our miracle.

the Healer to receive his miracle — and on the other side of his miracle, Bartimaeus had a new identity. Now he was a follower of Jesus who could see everything!

So what came in between "blind Bartimaeus" and "seeing Bartimaeus"? *His faith to seize his moment.*

What came in between "blind Bartimaeus" and "seeing Bartimaeus"? *His faith to seize his moment.*

Our place of faith is just as real as both the place of our problem and the place of our miracle!

Blind Bartimaeus had an opportunity to give up. We don't know how long he had to yell at Jesus before he got the Master's attention. We don't know how long those other people were criticizing him, ridiculing him, and telling him to shut up. But for blind Bartimaeus, it didn't matter. He was going to *stay* in that place of faith and keep on shouting and pursuing Jesus until he got His attention and stood before Him — right in the place of his miracle.

LAY HOLD OF *YOUR* MOMENT!

And God doesn't just perform a miracle for one. He does it for the benefit of those who will hear about it too. He knows that the power of a miracle will continue to work through the testimony of the one who received that miracle.

I told you previously about my story of suffering from that terrible skin disease for 13 years. After all I had gone through with that disease for all those years, it was easy to conclude, *Well, I guess this is my lot in life.*

But then I heard that radio preacher say, "By His stripes you're healed" — and when I heard it, something happened: Hope came into my heart.

I heard the preacher say, "Just start confessing that by His stripes you're healed." Well, from then on, I began to lay hold of my moments to give voice to my faith! I started singing over and over, "By His stripes I'm healed!" And I just kept saying all the time: "By His stripes I'm healed; by His stripes I'm healed!"

But as I explained, I didn't see anything happen right away. Weeks and months went by, and I just kept confessing that I was healed by the stripes of Jesus. Then one night, I went to bed just as I had gone to bed for 13 years with this horrible disease. And when I woke up the next morning and went to the mirror like I always did, my face was completely clear! There wasn't one blemish or sore on my forehead, my cheeks, or my neck — *nothing*!

That's why I have such conviction about wanting to see the work of the Miracle Worker in *your* life. The Holy Spirit doesn't want you to just say, "Oh, yes, Jesus is the Miracle Worker in Matthew, Mark, Luke, and John." No, He wants you to *know* beyond a shadow of a doubt: "Jesus is *my* Miracle Worker!"

Then should you ever experience a physical attack in your body and your brain tells you, *Oh, this is bad. Oh, this is serious* — you won't start planning your funeral right then and there the way some people do. Instead, you'll *seize* that moment to declare in faith, "*No, no, no!* That is *not* the way this is going to go! Jesus is my *Healer*, and by faith I receive my miracle!"

Remember — the same blood Jesus spilled and the suffering He went through to *save* you also *healed* you. He is your Savior, but He is also your *Healer.* He is a miracle-working God, so make the decision today that you *will* lay hold of *your* moment for a miracle!

PART 2

◆

HEAVEN'S KEYS TO UNLOCK YOUR HEALING

8

~

THE POWER OF FORGIVENESS

As I told you at the beginning of this book, I believe we need to build a strong foundation in our lives concerning divine healing in these *last of the last* days. Through the years as I have studied the Word in this area of healing, I have come to realize that there are certain key elements of our Christian walk that are directly tied to our physical healing. As we cultivate these spiritual principles in our walk with God, they will become powerful forces in our lives that will help bring health not only to our bodies, but to every area of our lives.

That's what this section of the book is all about. I want to share these precious keys of truth from God's Word to help you unlock your own healing as you meditate on them and make them a part of your everyday walk with Jesus.

BECOME A STRONG FORGIVER!

First, I want to talk to you about the power of forgiveness. It's so important that we become strong forgivers in these last days.

This is to be our identity as children of God: We are not those who hold on to an offense; rather, we extend forgiveness in every situation.

Paul prophesied in Second Timothy 3 about the time we're living in now, and one thing he wrote was that there would be more opportunities for relational problems in these last days. So if we want to lie down at night in peace, we need to be good forgivers.

It's so important that we become strong forgivers in these last days. This is to be our identity as children of God: We are not those who hold on to an offense; rather, we extend forgiveness in every situation.

I have such a passion for this subject, because I suffered for a few years with bitterness in my heart. You may ask, "How could that happen? You're a minister!" Well, it happened. It was several decades ago, but it was such a traumatic time in my life. Through that experience, I learned that bitterness and offense are absolutely as dangerous as carrying cancer around in our bodies.

Seeds of offense had been planted in my heart, but I didn't know it. And even if I had realized that I was harboring offense, I wouldn't have known how to get rid of it. At that time, I didn't know the principles I'm about to share with you. In fact, I just thought this person who had offended me needed to change so I could be fine again. Meanwhile, the offense grew into bitterness, and bitterness gradually extended its tentacles down into my soul and affected my personality.

It was like I had a trap over my mind. I'd go to bed thinking about how that person should change and how hurt I was, and I'd wake up in the morning with the same thoughts.

After a while, my hands and feet began to feel painfully cold all the time; then my face became cold. Fear continually tried to grip my mind. I even had panic attacks. It was so horrible. On three separate occasions in three different buildings, I thought the walls were closing in on me. Fear would speak and say, *"You're losing your mind."* But I didn't want to go to a doctor because I didn't want him to pronounce some terrible sentence on me.

The only way that I could get my mind and my body to settle down was to get by myself and start praising God. I'd set my eyes, my mind, and my heart on the Word of God every day, seeking for answers. I knew that He was my answer, but I didn't know what that looked like in this desperate situation.

Throughout this ordeal, I didn't even know that I was harboring bitterness. Our family — Rick and I and Paul, Philip, and Joel — traveled together in a car for two months all around the United States. It should have been a happy time of itinerating in ministry, but I was struggling inwardly every day.

Draw Near to God To Receive His Answers

But God gave us a promise in James 4:8 — that as we draw near to Him, He will draw near to us. And God is not a man that He should lie (*see* Numbers 23:19)! So what does God bring with Him when He draws near to us? He lovingly draws near with answers, with power, and with deliverance.

I was actually surprised by His answer to me during that difficult time period. As I drew near to Him, I'd start by asking, "Lord, could You please change this person and change this situation?"

But in those times of my drawing near to the Lord, He kept directing me to the truth that *I* was the one who needed to change. So I thought, *Well, if I'm going to change, I need to draw even closer to God.*

So I'm just telling you how I did it. I began to sacrifice my sleep. I'd get up earlier than my family, and every morning I'd spend an hour with God. I was seeking hard after Him, but I didn't feel like I was getting any better or that I was getting any answers.

> God doesn't lie, and He said if I draw near to Him, He's going to draw near to me. I was the one with the questions and the need, so I kept doing all I knew to draw close to Him by spending time with Him every day.

But, you see, God doesn't lie, and He said if I draw near to Him, He's going to draw near to me. I was the one with the questions and the need, so I kept doing all I knew to draw close to Him by spending time with Him every day.

Sometimes people just want someone to pray for them and make everything all right in their lives. And it's true that at times when people have someone lay hands on them and pray, the power of God causes a miraculously quick work to take place.

But God loves you so much that He wants you to know Him,

and the only way you can get to know someone is to spend time with that person. So if you want to draw close to God and receive all He desires to give you, you must make time for Him.

There have been times through the years when I've wanted to be close to God and sense His presence as I prayed, but I couldn't. I'd ask Him, *Lord, what is it?* And for me, His answer was often right in line with what we're talking about: I had offense in my heart.

Our heart can be likened to a pipe that God's Spirit wants to flow through. But unforgiveness is one of the key things in life that can clog up our "pipe," making the Word of God unfruitful in our lives and causing us not to be sensitive to His voice.

One thing that can help us greatly in becoming more sensitive to the Holy Spirit as we draw near to the Lord is to pray in other tongues.

But you, beloved, building yourselves up on your most holy faith, praying in the Holy Spirit.

Jude 20

So as you draw near to God and you pray in the Spirit, it's like you're charging your inner "battery." As you begin to quiet your mind and pray in tongues, it causes you to switch your focus. You are accessing another realm and touching what is eternal inside you. You are building up your faith, which works by love (*see* Galatians 5:6), and that love is strengthening your relationship with Jesus, making you more aware of His will for your life — including His desire for you to forgive those who have offended you.

You may even have to forgive someone, or affirm your forgiveness, multiple times a day. But there is something wonderful about that, because every time you choose to forgive, you're saying no to the devil and yes to God! You're saying, "Devil, you're not taking my joy; you're not taking my strength. I'm going to forgive and pray for that person, and that is going to open the door to Heaven in my life!"

'I'M NOT LETTING GO OF YOU!'

So I drew as close to Jesus as I could during this very scary time in my life. I remember one night during a particular ministry trip.

As you begin to quiet your mind and pray in tongues, it causes you to switch your focus. You are accessing another realm and touching what is eternal inside you. You are building up your faith, which works by love.

We were staying in a hotel, and in the middle of the night, the mental torment became so great that I couldn't sleep. I got out of bed, and at one point, I just took hold of the bathroom sink with both hands in desperation and quietly spoke these words out loud: "God, I don't know what You want, and I don't know what to do or how to change, *but I'm not letting go of You.*"

I was determined: I was *not* going to quit seeking God, even though at that time, I saw no remedy for the situation. But something shifted inside my soul at that point.

Two weeks later, we were in a ministry meeting, and a prophet of God came up to me and said, "You're a very sensitive person, but you have broken places on the inside of you." Then he added, *"In 24 hours, you're going to wake up in a different world."*

And that is exactly what happened. Within 24 hours, the Lord enabled me to see my situation from the perspective of forgiveness. Before that moment, I didn't even know I needed to forgive. But after that prophet spoke to me, Jesus began to work in my heart and open my eyes to that truth, and I asked for forgiveness from my offender for my bitterness and resentment.

I went to bed, and the next morning when I opened my eyes, it was just like the prophet had said: *It was like I woke up in a different world.* My hands, my feet, and my mind were all absolutely normal. It was as if sometime in the middle of the night, Jesus had stuck His invisible hand into my heart and removed all the bitterness. I was completely delivered!

That's why I share this message with so much passion — because I know from hard experience that you and I simply cannot afford to live in offense. Bitterness not only opens the door to problems in our relationships, but it can also cause sickness and disease in our bodies. It's a poison that God does not want in our lives.

I know from hard experience that you and I simply cannot afford to live in offense. Bitterness not only opens the door to problems in our relationships, but it can also cause sickness and disease in our bodies.

FIRST THINGS FIRST: *FORGIVENESS*

I want you to see how important forgiveness is by showing you what happened between Jesus and His disciples when He came into their midst soon after He was raised from the dead.

In John 20:21, Jesus said to the disciples, "...Peace to you!" Then verse 22 goes on to say, "And when He had said this, He breathed on them, and said to them, 'Receive the Holy Spirit.'"

In that moment, the disciples were born again and received the indwelling Holy Spirit. It is significant to note the very next thing that Jesus said to them:

"If you forgive the sins of any, they are forgiven them; if you retain the sins of any, they are retained."

John 20:23

Jesus was notifying His disciples that they had just been granted the power to forgive and release people from any sin committed against them! He plainly said in this verse, "If you hold on to that offense, it will be retained." In other words, if the offender doesn't repent and we don't forgive, the sin of the offense remains on the offender. It's going to stay right there.

That verse also indicates that if someone sins against you and you refuse to forgive that person, you stay connected to that sin. The one who offended you could live on the other side of the world, and you could decide that you're never going to see that person again. Nevertheless, it will be as if there is an invisible string reaching across the earth to tie you to that offense, just like it happened yesterday.

But if we forgive, that person is released from the offense in the spirit realm — and that unseen realm is far more powerful than the natural realm. And we do even more when we forgive: As we set our offender free, we simultaneously free ourselves.

That's the good news Jesus presented in this verse: that not only can you be set free from all negative effects of that offense, but you can free your offender as well. Jesus said in this verse that if you forgive the offender, that person is forgiven and you have actually released that person from the offense.

How amazing to consider that forgiveness was the first principle of the Kingdom that Jesus wanted His disciples to understand in the moments right after they received the indwelling Holy Spirit. Immediately after they received the Helper whom Jesus had promised, He gave them instruction that they could only accomplish *with* that Helper: "If you hold on to another person's sin, it is retained; if you forgive, it is forgiven."

> How amazing to consider that forgiveness was the first principle of the Kingdom that Jesus wanted His disciples to understand in the moments right after they received the indwelling Holy Spirit.

THE CHURCH'S FIRST MARTYR TAUGHT US TO FORGIVE

Stephen was one of the first believers of the Early Church, and he had been preaching to the Jewish people. The Jewish elders accused him of blaspheming and hauled him before their council, where Stephen boldly presented a scriptural defense. Acts 7:54 says, "When they heard these things they were cut to the heart...."

When the Jewish elders heard the preaching of the Gospel, they became so angry that verse 54 says they gnashed at Stephen with their teeth. But even as they shouted for Stephen's stoning, Stephen had a vision of Jesus.

But he, being full of the Holy Spirit, gazed into heaven and saw the glory of God, and Jesus standing at the right hand of God, and said, "Look! I see the heavens opened and the Son of Man standing at the right hand of God!"

Acts 7:55,56

What Stephen saw in the Spirit was so real that he asked those present, "Can't you see it?" But that made the elders even angrier.

Then they cried out with a loud voice, stopped their ears, and ran at him with one accord; and they cast him out of the city and stoned him....

Acts 7:57,58

This is how the Jews executed judgment in New Testament times. They would take the one condemned outside the city and put the person in a pit, and people would throw huge stones upon the condemned until he or she was dead.

...And the witnesses laid down their clothes at the feet of a young man named Saul.

Acts 7:58

This young man named Saul was the future apostle Paul. Of course, Stephen didn't know that. Saul just looked like another one of the people screaming at him and wanting him dead.

From my husband Rick's studies of the original Greek, he has discovered how demon-possessed Saul was before he came to Jesus. Saul believed Christians were heretics and enjoyed watching Christians scream; he enjoyed seeing their blood flow. Saul was very sadistically zealous about apprehending them — men, women, and children — knowing that they would be horribly abused, imprisoned, and even killed. On that day when Stephen was hauled to the place of execution, Saul was one of those standing around the pit where they were stoning Stephen and was actually relishing the scene being played out before him (*see* Acts 22:20).

> **And they stoned Stephen as he was calling on God and saying, "Lord Jesus, receive my spirit."**
>
> Acts 7:59

Stephen was very close to entering Heaven, almost without breath left in his lungs.

> **Then he knelt down and cried out with a loud voice, "Lord, do not charge them with this sin." And when he had said this, he fell asleep.**
>
> Acts 7:60

With the last breath in Stephen's lungs, he cried out to God that the people responsible for his death would be forgiven, saying, "Lord, do not charge them with this sin." Stephen was freeing those present from the consequences of the great sin they were committing at that moment. And the future apostle Paul was in that crowd. At the time, he was a very cruel man named Saul of Tarsus, who was enjoying his role as a witness to Stephen's death.

But with Stephen's last breath, he freed them all! Stephen cried out for God's forgiveness, and in that split second, every person in that crowd was released from the sin they were committing against him — including Saul of Tarsus.

ADOPTING GOD'S PERSPECTIVE OF OUR OFFENDERS

With that in mind, remember what Jesus said in John 20:23:

"If you forgive the sins of any, they are forgiven them; if you retain the sins of any, they are retained."

When I started studying this subject of forgiveness, I came to this account of Stephen's martyrdom and read how Stephen freed all those people from the sin they committed against him. In light of Jesus' words in John 20:23, I thought to myself, *What if Stephen had not forgiven? Would we have had an apostle Paul?* Under the inspiration of the Holy Spirit, Paul wrote more than two-thirds of the New Testament. Would we have the New Testament epistles that Paul wrote if Stephen hadn't released Saul of Tarsus from the sin he participated in that day?

Then my next question was to myself: *When I don't forgive someone, what kind of blessing or divine call am I perhaps stopping that person from fulfilling?*

Now, of course we don't know the answer to my unspoken question — whether we would even have had an apostle Paul if Stephen hadn't forgiven him and all those present. But we do know that Jesus said, in essence, "Those whose sins you forgive, they are forgiven, and those whose sins you retain, they are retained." From just that one verse, we know we have a great responsibility to forgive.

We see our ultimate Example in Luke 23:34 as Jesus hung on the Cross, bearing the sin of the whole world. As His precious blood poured out of His body and He suffered pain beyond what you and I could ever comprehend, Jesus cried out: "Father, forgive them! They don't know what they're doing." With those words, Jesus forgave all those involved in His cruel torture and death.

Now, if you and I had been there, we might have protested, "Of course they know what they are doing!" But according to

God's perspective, they *didn't* actually know what they were doing — and Jesus said, "Forgive them, Father."

So this is God's perspective of forgiveness. This is how we get free — by taking stock of whatever wrongs were done to us and then saying, "Father, those who hurt or offended me didn't know what they were doing. Do not charge them with this sin." That frees both the offenders and us!

We see in Matthew 18:21 what Jesus had to say about forgiveness. The conversation started with Peter, who was always speaking out. I can just imagine that he thought he really had the right answer to Jesus' question.

> **Then Peter came to Him and said, "Lord, how often shall my brother sin against me, and I forgive him? Up to seven times?"**
>
> **Matthew 18:21**

Peter probably thought, *That was a great answer I just gave to Jesus.* Seven times was certainly more than anyone could be expected to forgive a repeat offender!

But look at how Jesus responded to Peter:

> **…"I do not say to you, up to seven times, but up to seventy times seven."**
>
> **Matthew 18:22**

Jesus was saying, "You have to forgive one another until *infinity!* In other words, there is no limit to the number of times you must forgive someone."

DON'T HOLD YOUR OFFENDER CAPTIVE

Then Jesus began to teach on forgiveness using a powerful parable.

> **"Therefore the kingdom of heaven is like a certain king who wanted to settle accounts with his servants. And when he had begun to settle accounts, one was brought to him who owed him ten thousand talents."**
>
> **Matthew 18:23,24**

Ten thousand talents is the equivalent today of ten million dollars! That is a lot of money — a huge debt — and the servant just didn't have the ability to pay it.

> **"But as he was not able to pay, his master commanded that he be sold, with his wife and children and all that he had, and that payment be made. The servant therefore fell down before him, saying, 'Master, have patience with me, and I will pay you all.' Then the master of that servant was moved with compassion, released him, and forgave him the debt."**
>
> **Matthew 18:25-27**

The master forgave the servant that huge debt. That's just like our story with God. All of us owed Him a great debt. The Bible says that *all* have sinned and come short of the glory of God (*see* Romans 3:23). It's a debt that none of us could pay. We couldn't do enough good deeds. We couldn't give away enough money or sacrifice enough time. None of those things could pay our debt. We owed that debt, but if we've been born again, we have been *forgiven* that debt.

In Jesus' parable, in the same way, the master forgave the servant of a debt he simply could not pay. But let's look at his response to the huge debt he'd been forgiven.

> **"But that servant went out and found one of his fellow servants who owed him a hundred denarii; and he laid hands on him and took him by the throat, saying, 'Pay me what you owe!'"**
>
> **Matthew 18:28**

The debt of the fellow servant was the equivalent of approximately 20 dollars. So this man who had been forgiven *10 million dollars* was demanding that his fellow servant pay him the *20 dollars* that was owed to him!

You would think that someone who had been forgiven so much would forgive another who owed him such a small debt. But this servant who had been forgiven so much wrapped his hands around the fellow servant's throat and said, "Pay me what you owe me!"

> **So his fellow servant fell down at his feet and begged him, saying, "Have patience with me, and I will pay you all."**
>
> **Matthew 18:29**

This servant who owed 20 dollars asked for mercy and patience — which is exactly what the first servant did who had been forgiven a great debt. But the first servant would not forgive the small debt of his fellow servant the way his own master had forgiven him. Instead, the servant put this man in prison for a debt of 20 dollars!

And he would not, but went and threw him into prison till he should pay the debt.

Matthew 18:30

Jesus was emphasizing the very thing that we are *not* to do when someone commits an offense against us. We are not to hold that person captive to that offense through our own unforgiveness.

And his master was angry, and delivered him to the torturers until he should pay all [the ten million dollars] **that was due to him.**

Matthew 18:34

Then in verse 35, we read Jesus' sober warning: "So My heavenly Father also will do to you if each of you, from his heart, does not forgive his brother his trespasses."

A TESTIMONY OF FORGIVENESS

I want to share a story that really happened and that explains so well this principle of forgiveness in our day and time.

Several years ago, I met a woman who was serving in the church. When I began to talk to her, we really connected. She told me that she had a son and that the man she was currently with was her second husband.

I said, "Well, tell me, how did you get over the pain of your relationship with your first husband?"

She replied, "Oh, my first husband was terrible. He was an abusive alcoholic, and he would often hit our son, which caused our son mental problems. Finally, I divorced my husband. It was some time after the divorce that I learned about Jesus and got saved. Ever since, I have loved Jesus with all my heart.

"Later I married my second husband, who is a wonderful man, but I carried into my second marriage the unresolved offenses of my first marriage. I started accusing my second husband of things he wasn't even guilty of that my first husband used to do.

"I told the Lord, 'God, I know this is wrong. Please free me from this bitterness. I know I have to forgive that man.'"

Making that process more difficult was the fact that she also had to deal with the mental problems of her son that had resulted from his father's abuse on a daily basis for many years.

This woman was seeking the Lord one day as she was cleaning to move out of her apartment into another apartment. She had succeeded in getting all the trash in one place and was almost ready to put it all into bags and get rid of it all. She looked at the pile of trash and thought with relief, *Oh, I'm almost done!*

Then she looked over to her right and saw a tiny piece of paper lying separate from the pile of trash. As she was getting ready to sweep that little piece of paper over into the big pile, the Holy Spirit spoke to her spirit, saying, *"Do you see this huge pile of trash? That's like the debt you owed Me. And do you see this little tiny piece of paper? That's like the debt your ex-husband owes you."*

What a revelation! In that powerful moment, this woman was able to forgive her first husband and set him free from the prison built by his offenses against her and their son. And in forgiving, this woman set *herself* free as well from the bitterness that had been working its terrible effects within her body, mind, and emotions for so long — and her freedom then impacted her current

---

marriage. Her relationship with her husband began to grow closer —
and her son's mental condition was healed!

UNLOCK THE PRISON DOOR

Friend, the truth is, your offenders do owe you a debt. What
they did to you was real; the pain you suffered because of those
offenses is real. They owe you a debt, but they cannot pay it.

Just as we couldn't pay the debt of sin we owed to God, others
who have sinned against us can't pay the debt they owe us. So how
do they get free?

Let's go back to our story of the servant who was forgiven
so much. He decides not to forgive the small debt of his fellow
servant. Instead, he throws the man in prison, slams the prison
door, and puts the key in his pocket. Then he walks away, saying,
"I'm sure glad *I'm* free!"

But the truth is, that first servant *isn't* really free, because he
has left a man in prison, whom he had the power to set free.

You and I have been forgiven a debt — one that we could
never repay. What are we supposed to do for those who hurt us?
They owe us a debt, and we are the ones with the key. We have to
take the key out of our pocket, use it to open the prison door, and
let our offenders out. We have to set them free.

I know of one young woman who hadn't spoken to her father
for 32 years because of past offenses. After forgiving her father,
she called him. She didn't talk to him about what he had done
to her. She just said, "Please forgive me, Father," and he started
crying and responded, "Forgive *me*."

The devil wanted to continue to destroy that bond between father and daughter. But the love of God in that young woman's heart had the power to help her forgive her dad and restore that relationship.

This is God's will for each one of us — that we are people who *forgive*. God wants to restore relationships, not destroy them, and you and I hold the key to setting our offenders free. Even if the other person feels no penitence for his or her actions and restoration isn't possible, we can open the way for that other person to walk free and in the process walk completely free ourselves.

What are we supposed to do for those who hurt us? They owe us a debt, and we are the ones with the key. We have to take the key out of our pocket, use it to open the prison door, and let our offenders out. We have to set them free.

SUPERNATURAL EQUIPMENT
THAT EMPOWERS US TO FORGIVE

You might be thinking, *But you don't know what they did to me.* And that is true. But I know that you hold the key to their prison, and you're the one who can set them free.

You see, Jesus wouldn't ask us to forgive if He hadn't given us the needed equipment to obey His command. He has given us the *agape* love of God. The Holy Spirit has poured God's love into our hearts, and we are well able to set our offenders free (*see* Romans 5:5).

In Second Corinthians 10, Paul wrote about our supernatural equipment to pull down strongholds, including strongholds in our mind of bitterness and unforgiveness.

For the weapons of our warfare are not carnal but mighty in God for pulling down strongholds.

2 Corinthians 10:4

Your weapons that enable you to walk in love and forgiveness are not carnal, but they are *powerful* to pull down the enemy's strongholds. So what are those weapons? You find them in verse 5: "Casting down arguments and every high thing that exalts itself against the knowledge of God, bringing *every thought into captivity to the obedience of Christ.*"

You are not to allow thoughts of anger and bitterness to dominate your mind. You have to cast them down and bring those thoughts into submission to what the Word of God says.

So when a bitter thought comes, what are you going to do? Just let it stay in your mind where you can meditate on it and allow it to become even more deeply embedded in your life? Not if you want to be free from it! You have to take every wrong thought *captive.* That's exactly what the Bible says. It says you have to bring *"every thought into captivity to the obedience of Christ."*

We are the ones responsible to do this. *We* bring those wrong thoughts down. We have the authority of the name of Jesus. We have the power of the blood of Jesus. We have a covenant with Almighty God. The Spirit of God lives inside us!

So just do what the Bible tells you to do! Say, "No, devil — I'm casting down that thought of bitterness and unforgiveness.

I forgive that person, and I release him (or her) from every offense committed against me in the name of Jesus!"

Continue to do that over and over again every time similar thoughts try to come to your mind and you feel tempted to dwell on them. As you consistently cast down every wrong thought concerning those who have offended you, you are eliminating every stronghold of unforgiveness that tries to set up camp in your mind. You have the power to bring those strongholds down!

You are not to allow thoughts of anger and bitterness to dominate your mind. You have to cast them down and bring those thoughts into captivity to the obedience of Christ.

And you *must* do this. It's so important that you walk in forgiveness, both for your spiritual and your physical health. In fact, the Bible says that if we don't forgive, God won't forgive us (*see* Mark 11:25)!

As I mentioned before, Scripture also says that we have the power to forgive because the love of God has been shed abroad in our hearts by the Holy Ghost (*see* Romans 5:5). So it's not your goodness or your great personality that enables you to forgive; it's the love of God inside of you.

If there are people you need to forgive, I invite you to pray this prayer right now.

Father, I ask You not to charge these individuals with the sins they committed against me. Father, please forgive

them; they didn't know what they were doing. **Right now I choose to forgive each one. I set them free from the prison where I have held them captive through my unforgiveness. And, Lord, I ask You to forgive me for holding on to offense. Please cleanse me by Your blood in the name of Jesus. Amen.**

As you consistently cast down every wrong thought concerning those who have offended you, you are eliminating every stronghold of unforgiveness that tries to set up camp in your mind. You have the power to bring those strongholds down!

If you prayed that prayer, you may need to contact someone — make a phone call or write a note, an email, etc. Remember, you're the one with the key. Your offender is likely carrying the shame and guilt of what he or she did to you. But with the love of God, you can set that person free.

This message of forgiveness is so important when it comes to the subject of healing, because bitterness has been the source of countless physical afflictions in people's bodies over the centuries. In these last days we're living in, God is clearing away every obstacle that keeps us from fulfilling our destinies as we live out our lives in Him healed and whole. That's why He gives us the key of forgiveness. It's time to unlock some prison doors!

9

THE POWER OF CONTROLLING YOUR EMOTIONS

Things are happening in our world that tell us the time is near for Jesus' return. Never has it been more important for us to keep our spirit man strong and in control of our emotions.

You have probably seen someone in your life who absolutely lost control of his or her emotions. Maybe that person yelled, screamed, or even cursed at someone you loved, and you said to yourself, *I don't ever want to be like that.* Or maybe *you* were that person who got in a situation where you lost control of your emotions and then felt terrible about it later.

Emotions are a gift from God and a blessing, but it has never been His will that we would be controlled by our emotions. God has provided wisdom for us to learn how to control our emotions, which is a vital part of what we need to do to receive our healing and live in divine health.

WE *CAN* CONTROL OUR EMOTIONS

The Bible says that we were created in God's image (*see* Genesis 1:26,27). God has emotions, and so do we. Emotions in themselves are not bad; it's what we do with them that makes them good or bad.

Many people have a false picture of God painted in their minds. They assume that He is often angry and out to destroy us. For instance, society has a term for natural disasters, such as tornadoes or hurricanes, that can wreak havoc on the earth: They are often called "acts of God." But that's a lie of the devil, because those weather events are *not* initiated by God.

God does have emotion. Zephaniah 3:17 shows us that He experiences joy.

> **The Lord your God in your midst, the Mighty One, will save; He will rejoice over you with gladness, He will quiet you with His love....**

God has so much gladness and joy that this word "rejoice" in the Hebrew includes the meaning of *spinning*. God doesn't just rejoice over you; He dances in delight over you! That's how much He loves you. He feels great joy and compassion when He thinks of you.

Jesus is the express image of God, and when Jesus was soon to be crucified, at one point He looked over Jerusalem and said, "O Jerusalem, Jerusalem, the one who kills the prophets and stones those who are sent to her! How often I wanted to gather your children together, as a hen gathers her chicks under her wings, but you were not willing!" (Matthew 23:37). We can sense the great emotion in Jesus' words.

So we know from God's Word that there is nothing wrong with our emotions; however, we don't want to be controlled by them. The Bible says be angry, but to sin not (*see* Ephesians 4:26). So anger in itself is not a sin; it's what we do with that anger. If we yell and scream and curse at someone because we are angry, then we have allowed this emotion to move us into fleshly action. Emotion has great power, and it can move us to do the wrong thing if we let it.

Anger is normal, but we need to control it. That's what this chapter is about, because controlling our emotions is vital to our physical health.

You might be saying to yourself, *I can't control my emotions. I listened to my mother scream for so many years of my life. I heard my father's angry cursing throughout my years growing up. Now I'm just doing what my parents did. I can't help it.*

If you're saying that, I want to tell you that it's not true. You *can* help it. When God says, "Be angry and sin not," He's telling us what to do. He would never tell us to do something that He didn't equip us to do, because He is just and completely fair. God has given us the equipment we need to control our emotions. So how can we train ourselves, and what has the Holy Spirit already done to help us?

God has given us the equipment we need to control our emotions. So how can we train ourselves, and what has the Holy Spirit already done to help us?

The word "emotions" comes from a Middle French word that means *to move, to shake, to stir, to set in motion,* or *to move the feelings.* When our emotions start to rise and push their way to the forefront to speak in our lives, we can feel the power of their motion — but the Bible says we can control them.

Our emotions can cause us to feel sad, happy, excited, energized, fearful, confused, or depressed — and that's just the beginning of the range of those powerful emotions that can potentially move us, stir us, and exert their influence on us. Our emotions can also change quickly. One minute we can feel happiness, and five minutes later, we may hear something upsetting that someone said or a negative thought may enter our mind — and suddenly our emotions have moved us into a state of sadness.

So it's a powerful strength to be able to control our emotions. I want to give myself as an example, even though it's not an example I'm proud of.

Many years ago after the fall of the Iron Curtain when we were living in Latvia, I was being dominated and controlled by fear. I had allowed the enemy to paint all sorts of terrible imaginations in my mind, and I became fearful that someone was going to bring harm to me. As a result, I would try to control my environment so I wouldn't be alone and I could therefore stay safe.

I remember one day when our eldest son Paul, who was about nine or ten years old at the time, said to me, "Mom, come to the store with me."

I said, "No, Paul, I don't think I'm going to go."

Why did I say no? Because I was afraid that there was someone parked outside the store who was going to bring harm to us. I was being controlled by fear that had been generated by a vain imagination — and in that moment, that fear dominated my mind and stole the fun time I could have had with my son.

At the time, I didn't have the spiritual maturity I have now. I haven't arrived, but I have grown. I didn't know that I could speak to myself and take control over that negative emotion of fear. I didn't know that I could have told myself, *Denise, that's ridiculous. Take authority over fear right now in the name of Jesus, and then go out there and enjoy your son!* As a result, that fear dominated me, moving me into actions that said *no* to a needed time of fellowship with my son.

But Jesus went right to the root of this issue of fear with His own blood! When He was on the Cross, He cried out, "It is finished!" The work Jesus completed on the Cross as the blood poured from His body was for you and me to be free from all mental torment on this earth, and that includes fear.

Thank God for the anointing that crushes and destroys the yoke of bondage (*see* Isaiah 10:27). I pray you reach out and take this truth and make it a reality for yourself. Just receive that Jesus is the Answer. I speak freedom from fear to you in the powerful name of the Lord Jesus Christ!

> Jesus went right to the root of this issue of fear with His own blood! When He was on the Cross, He cried out, "It is finished!" The work Jesus completed on the Cross as the blood poured from His body was for you and me to be free from all mental torment on this earth, and that includes fear.

HOW TO KEEP YOUR SPIRIT MAN
IN CONTROL OF YOUR EMOTIONS

So when our emotions are knocking at the door, how can we answer the door in a way that brings light and help to us? How do we ensure that our spirit man stays in control of our emotions?

Let's consider what we can do when we're angry. We can either speak to ourselves, or we can listen to that emotion and allow it to move us to an emotional state that isn't good. We might start yelling and screaming at someone, or we might block our heart from that person, telling ourselves, *I'll never forgive him (or her) for this.* If that's the choice we make and we allow that powerful emotion of anger to move us and cause us to sin, I guarantee you that this kind of reaction will have a detrimental effect on our bodies.

But there's an answer for those of us who are Christians. We're not supposed to be led around by our emotions or to allow our emotions to control us. We shouldn't be screaming and yelling at people. We are not at liberty to give people a piece of our carnal mind or to threaten people with negative consequences for not pleasing us!

So what is our answer? We are to take the time to ask the Holy Spirit who dwells within us for wisdom.

The heart of the righteous studies how to answer, but the mouth of the wicked pours forth evil.

Proverbs 15:28

Do you see the two choices in this verse? We either study how to answer, or we pour forth out of our mouths what is evil. The Holy Spirit is so personal, and when we fall into these kinds of emotionally upsetting situations, He is there to give us the help we need if we will take the time to ask Him for that help.

So let's say that you're in a disagreement with someone and you realize it is becoming a "heated" argument. I believe it would be wise to politely ask to be excused and then to remove yourself from the presence of that argument. Then you need to "study" — consider or think carefully — how to answer before you return to that conversation.

It might help to ask yourself the following questions:

- *Am I losing control of my emotions?*

- *What good is going to come out of this argument if I continue?*

- *Is this subject worth the unrest and strife it's causing? Will it still matter in five years?*

- *What damage am I going to do if I continue?*

- *Should I wait to say more until I've prayed and received God's wisdom on how to approach this subject in love and at the right time?*

- *Do I need to ask forgiveness for my part in what has already been said?*

These are questions we can ask ourselves. This is what the scripture means when it says to *study* how to answer. It's so practical!

God's counsel is the most practical instruction we will find anywhere. He gives us words of wisdom in His Word, and if we are wise, we will incline our ears and *listen* to what He is telling us. Wisdom is saying: *I don't have to be controlled by my emotions. I can take control myself. I can study how to answer, and I can keep evil from pouring out of my mouth.* Conducting your behavior in this manner is the wisdom of God.

YOUR 'SECRET WEAPON' LIVES INSIDE YOU

And you don't have to study how to answer on your own. If you're a Christian, the Holy Spirit lives inside you (*see* 1 Corinthians 3:16)! Think of it — the Third Person of the Godhead, the Lover of your soul, the One who knows you better than you know yourself — dwells within your spirit!

The Holy Spirit is your Helper and your Guide (*see* John 15:26; 16:13,14). He has the perfect answer for your problem. He isn't a "cookie-cutter" Holy Spirit who has the same answer for everyone. He has the exact right answer for *you.* He's personal to you. He knows your situation, and He has answers with your name on them!

He isn't a "cookie-cutter" Holy Spirit who has the same answer for everyone. He knows your situation, and He has answers with your name on them!

This wonderful Counselor and Guide is never going to leave you (*see* John 14:16). He knows what you're going to say before you say it. He hears your thoughts before you think them (*see* Psalm 139:2-4). And He has perfect help available just for you.

So when you get into a situation and your emotions are trying to move you into fear, anger, or confusion — just remember that the Holy Spirit has been assigned to you in order to help you. Jesus has made sure of it!

Before Jesus laid down His life, He had some final things to say to His disciples. He loved them so much. They had been with Him every day for three years, and such a close relationship had been cultivated. Jesus told them, "Don't let your heart be troubled. I'm going to leave you, but I won't leave you to live as orphans. I'm sending you the Holy Spirit!" (*see* John 14:1,18).

Jesus was talking not only to the disciples at that moment; He was also talking to you and me. You see, when we turn to the Holy Spirit for help and receive His comfort, those wrong emotions begin to subside. We turn our situation over to God and say, "Holy Spirit, this is bad; please help me. I don't know what to do with my anger right now." Or we say, "Holy Spirit, I'm so fearful in this situation. Please help me."

As we open our heart to the Holy Spirit and ask for His help, He rushes to bring His comfort and guidance to us. Remember, Jesus promised, "I'm not going to leave you. I'm sending One to you who is just like Me."

OVERCOMERS EVEN IN TRIBULATION

We won't have perfect lives while living on this earth. We will face obstacles that we will need to overcome by faith, and at times those obstacles may include physical sickness or infirmities. But in the midst of it all, Jesus gave us these powerful words of encouragement to sustain and to strengthen us:

"These things I have spoken to you, that in Me you may have peace. In the world you will have tribulation; but be of good cheer, I have overcome the world."

John 16:33

Now, that is a powerful promise. In this world, we are going to have tribulation, but in Jesus, we have peace that surpasses natural understanding (*see* Philippians 4:6,7). As we face situations that seem impossible, it might take us a little while until we experience His peace. Things that we simply wish weren't happening can press on our minds and hearts. But what can we do? Jesus told us in that verse. He said, "In Me, you can have peace."

My life is not a perfect life, and, yes, at times I've had to deal with physical and emotional challenges. But one thing I know — it is in Jesus that I find my peace.

After Jesus promised us His peace, He went on to promise something else: "…In the world you will have tribulation…" (John 16:33). Why is Jesus promising us this? Because He knows something about this world. He knows something about people. But even though Jesus says that we will have tribulation in this world, He also says, "…Be of good cheer, I have overcome the world."

As we serve Jesus faithfully even through a time of experiencing tribulation, we're showing the strength of our faith. When everything is going great, it seems like we don't even have to use our faith. It's when we're in those hard places and we might be tempted to give up that the real test comes.

We have to let our spirit man rise up and take control of our emotions in those times. We have to look to Heaven and say, "Jesus, I'm *not* giving up. This trial isn't easy to go through, but I know this: You are good, and You are faithful. And no matter what I'm going through, I'm trusting You to bring me out on the other side!"

Always remember these words of Jesus, because you're going to need them in this life. Jesus said that tribulation comes to everyone, which means you're not exempt. But He also said that in Him, you will find strength in His abiding peace. And then He said, "Cheer up — because here is the bottom line: I have overcome the world, and that overcoming power is in you!"

That overcoming power comes in the Person of the Holy Spirit, who promises to do exceedingly abundantly above all you could ever ask or think. He works in you with the same power that raised Jesus from the dead (*see* Romans 8:11; Ephesians 1:19,20; 3:20). That means you are *well* able to take control of your emotions so that they work *for* you and not *against* you. Wholeness in every area of your life — spirit, soul, and body — that is the will of God for you!

Jesus said that tribulation comes to everyone, which means you're not exempt. And then He said, "Cheer up — because here is the bottom line: I have overcome the world, and that overcoming power is in you!"

10

~

THE POWER OF JOY

The power of joy comes from the Greater One on the inside of us. It's greater than any depression, any oppression, or any physical symptoms that can come against us. This joy is so powerful that it will push all those hindrances out of the way, because the joy of the Lord is a conquering joy!

I want to tell you my story about joy, because when I was growing up, my dad would say, "Well, here comes the bear to the breakfast table." He said that because I could lean toward being a dramatic, melancholic personality. At times I'd walk about with a serious and somewhat sad attitude, especially in the morning.

However, as I grew up, I started to see that my tendency to lean toward melancholy was not a blessing to anyone. God started speaking to my heart about it. One day He said this to me: "My Word says, 'This is the day the Lord has made; we will rejoice and be glad in it'" (*see* Psalm 118:24).

I thought, *That one verse has a lot in it.* I began to meditate on that verse. This very day that you and I are living in right now was created by God — and He has *commanded* us to rejoice and be glad in it. It's a command! It's not a tentative option: "Well, I *might* rejoice." No, it's a firm and definite decision to obey God: "I *will* rejoice and be glad!"

This very day that you and I are living in right now was created by God — and He has *commanded* us to rejoice and be glad in it. It's not a tentative option: "Well, I *might* rejoice." No, it's a firm and definite decision to obey God: "I *will* rejoice and be glad!"

As I meditated on that scripture, I came to the conclusion: *Well, I just need to do better at this. Instead of dragging myself into the kitchen and saying in a monotone voice, "Well, hi, everybody," I need to have joy!*

So the next morning, I got out of bed, looked in the mirror, and said, "This is the day that the Lord has made. I will rejoice and be glad in it!" Then I said it again: "This is the day that the Lord has made. I will rejoice and be glad in it!"

I just kept repeating that scripture several times; then I smiled at myself in the mirror and headed out of my bedroom with a joyful demeanor. As I joined my family in the kitchen, I said brightly, "Good morning! How's everybody doing?" I experienced *joy* that morning — and many mornings after that!

What changed for me that day? I learned how to deliberately *choose* to have joy. I'm still not perfect at this, but that day I learned that joy is a choice. I *chose* to recognize that the Greater One who lives inside me is greater than he that is in the world (*see* 1 John 4:4) — and He wants to express Himself through us with powerful, conquering joy!

Bringing the Presence
of Conquering Joy

Maybe you're not where you need to be in your "joy walk." But you can be assured that Jesus is *never* discouraged when He looks at you. As I mentioned earlier, Zephaniah 3:17 says that He *rejoices* over you with gladness. When Jesus looks at you, He sees the precious Holy Spirit and the treasure of God's power living inside you. He sees you as a beautiful trophy of His grace, and He rejoices! And remember, that Hebrew word for "rejoice" carries the meaning of *spinning*. Jesus gets so excited about you that He spins around with joy!

This is one scriptural proof that Jesus isn't religious. He doesn't stand there and say in a monotone voice, "These are My children. They are wonderful." Oh, no, He is so thrilled that He spins around and dances with joy when He thinks of you! He doesn't look at you with sadness, worry, or concern. He doesn't think, *Oh, my, that one may not make it.* No, He looks at you with *joy.*

Jesus is never depressed, and we never need to be depressed either. After all, we have the power of the Greater One inside us — and the Greater One likes to express Himself through *joy.*

Have you ever been around someone who is always joyful? It either makes you want to become joyful like that person — or to slap the joy off the face of that person, because your own lack of joy is being revealed. That's what can happen, because joy is a conquering presence!

Someone with joy could come into the room where people are feeling discouraged and simply say, "Hey, guys, how is it going? It's going to be an awesome day!" And that person's words might encourage everyone in the room, because joy is a contagious,

> *Jesus is never depressed, and we never need to be depressed either. After all, we have the power of the Greater One inside us — and the Greater One likes to express Himself through joy.*

powerful, conquering force that has its source in the Greater One!

Psalm 45:7 says, "You love righteousness and hate wickedness; therefore God, Your God, has anointed You with the oil of gladness more than Your companions." That verse is talking about Jesus. Jesus had more joy than any of His companions while He walked on the earth. He was never depressed or sad because His disciples were messing up. Their mess-ups didn't bring Jesus down; He always walked in conquering joy.

We are called to follow Jesus' example in this realm of joy. When we or our loved ones are faced with sickness or physical challenges, we need to exercise the joy that's inside of us and allow His joy to be our strength (*see* Nehemiah 8:10). As we do, we will be an encouragement and a strength to people around us who are facing challenges.

We won't be one of those saying, "Oh, my, I can't believe this happened to you. This is horrible. This seems to keep happening to you. What are you going to do? There doesn't seem to be a solution for this problem." Instead, we will be able to impart strength to them through our joy and tell them with conviction and love, "It's going to be okay. This is not the end. God is faithful, and His Word is true!"

What kind of person would *you* rather be around when you're facing a bad report? I believe you would want someone who can bring the presence of conquering joy. You want one who will tell you, "I know you can get through this. You've been through other difficult situations. God was faithful to you then, and He'll be faithful to you now. I believe in you. God is in you, and you have the strength to come all the way through to the other side of this challenge. You're going to be okay."

Through the power of joy and by acting like the Greater One who lives inside you, you can bring joy into your situation and declare, "It's going to be okay!" Joy is so very, very powerful. Joy heals! The Bible says that a merry heart does good like a medicine (*see* Proverbs 17:22).

When we or our loved ones are faced with sickness or physical challenges, we need to exercise the joy that's inside of us and allow His joy to be our strength. As we do, we will be an encouragement and a strength to people around us who are facing challenges.

So if you're going through a physical challenge, just keep laughing and stay joyful! As you do, you're absolutely applying powerful medicine to your body. The truth is, you can completely change the situation through your joy!

I once watched a program in which a brain surgeon discussed his methods of helping his terminally ill patients. One method he described stood out to me: He actually sets aside rooms in which to place people who have life-threatening diseases. For a period of time, he gives them funny programs to watch that encourage them to laugh. The purpose of placing a patient in one of those rooms is to help that patient laugh and stir up joy.

How would even medical science know to do that? Because they know that joy heals. A merry heart truly does do good like a medicine! It heals your heart; and it can heal your body. Even modern scientists acknowledge the power of joy to heal.

JOY ISN'T DEPENDENT ON CIRCUMSTANCES

"Rejoice in the Lord always. Again I will say, rejoice!" (Philippians 4:4). Paul wrote those words while being held in prison, suffering in horrific conditions with raw sewage and death all around him. It was a *horrible* place to be. Yet it was there in that terrible prison that Paul wrote his letter to the church of Philippi and spoke of joy or rejoicing *at least 14 times* in four chapters!

If Paul could rejoice in that place of suffering, we can do the same in the midst of our challenges in life! We can let joy rise up and flow out as a conquering force as we acknowledge the Greater One who lives in us!

When joy comes forth from us, even in difficult situations, we know that it's not natural. The joy of the Holy Spirit we are releasing is a supernatural, conquering force that has the power to change circumstances! *That's* the kind of joy you and I have inside us!

One of the shortest verses in the Bible is about this conquering force of joy. It simply says, "Rejoice always" (1 Thessalonians 5:16). When are we to rejoice? Now and *always*! That is an amazing command that God expects us to obey. But, friend, we have the Greater One dwelling within to help us, and He expresses Himself through this beautiful fruit of conquering joy.

A Key That Unlocks Rejoicing

Now, I'm just like you. Sometimes I have a difficult time rejoicing. However, there is one key spiritual principle that helps me, and that is the act of giving thanks. When I start being thankful, my joy inevitably begins to increase.

It is impossible to be joyful and to complain at the same time. You're either going to be joyful, or you're going to complain. You're not going to find a complaining person who is joyful — but you're also not going to find a thankful person who is *not* joyful!

If you will just start thinking, even right now, *What do I have to be thankful for?* — that line of thinking will help you work up joy. The Greater One lives inside you, and His joy is one of the fruit of your born-again spirit. And He will help you stir up that joy as you deliberately start being thankful.

When I do this, I usually start by thanking the Lord for really simple things. I may start by thanking Him that I can see, that I can hear, and that I can walk. I thank Him for my husband, my family, and my friends. I thank Him that I have a house, food, and transportation.

When I start thanking the Lord, joy and thanksgiving start to rise up in my heart. I begin to say things such as, "Lord, thank You that You saved me. Thank You that

> You're either going to be joyful, or you're going to complain. You're not going to find a complaining person who is joyful — but you're also not going to find a thankful person who is *not* joyful!

You chose me. Thank You for the Holy Spirit who lives in me. Thank You for Your joy that is my strength!"

You see, friend, you have the power in you to say thank you, and it increases your joy. I'm choosing to be thankful, which increases my joy. And I acknowledge continually that I have the Greater One living inside me to help me.

If you are a believer in Jesus Christ, you have the Greater One inside you as well. He is greater than anything the enemy might try to bring against you, and He wants to express His power through you as the fruit of joy. Joy is so powerful.

One time years ago I was in an embarrassing situation when my mom came to visit us in Riga, Latvia, and she wanted me to sing on a downtown street. It was near Christmastime and we were walking in the city center. There were all kinds of people bustling around us, and then my mom said to me, "Denise, start singing."

I said, "Mom, I'm not going to start singing on the street."

Mom replied, "I want you to start singing."

Well, when your mom travels more than 5,000 miles to visit you and then keeps insisting, "Start singing," you're eventually going to start singing! At that moment, I had a headache, and I didn't feel well. But I did what my mom requested.

I stood there in Riga's city center and began singing. Soon a crowd began gathering to listen to me sing. I was so embarrassed by it all that I started laughing in the middle of my singing. But I was enjoying the look of joy on my mother's face. Then I realized that my headache had gone away! I felt fine, because joy has healing power. It's a medicine that brings healing to our bodies, which is exactly what the Bible says.

Do you need healing in your body today? If your answer is yes, then you need to smile. You need to laugh. You need to release joy! You can do that because of the presence of God inside you. That presence is more powerful than any outward symptoms in your body that you're dealing with.

He is the Greater One! He's greater than all those symptoms that are trying to claim your attention — and His joy can come pouring out of your spirit!

You can say, "Depression, I'm done with you! I'm going to laugh; I'm going to rejoice!"

Try doing what I did when I was first learning to release joy from the inside out. Go stand in front of a mirror and smile at yourself. Say out loud, "This is the day the Lord has made, and I will rejoice and be glad in it!" Then start making a practice of looking for things to be thankful for every day — and thank God for those things out loud! When you do that, you're acknowledging that the Word of God is true for *you*, and that's powerful!

Do you need healing in your body today? If your answer is yes, then you need to smile. You need to laugh. You need to release joy! You can do that because of the presence of God inside you. That presence is more powerful than any outward symptoms in your body that you're dealing with.

11

~

THE POWER OF
BEING THANKFUL

We talked briefly about the giving of thanks in the last chapter. But I want to talk to you further about the power of thankfulness. For us to be strong in every area of our lives in these last days, we need to be very thankful people.

Philippians 2:14 says, "Do all things without complaining and disputing." You simply can't complain and be thankful at the same time. It just doesn't work. You're either complaining or you're being thankful.

In this verse, the apostle Paul was telling us that complaining and disputing are not good for us. When we're complaining, we carry with us a negative atmosphere that affects everyone we come in contact with.

You may at times have been on the receiving end of this type of experience. Maybe you came into a setting where you were just so excited about and thankful for the goodness of God. But then someone else entered the room and started complaining, and his negative words changed the atmosphere.

The opposite of complaining is thankfulness, and Philippians 2:15 goes on to tell you how you can live in contrast to complainers and grumblers. When you're thankful, you become a blameless and harmless child of God, shining in the midst of a crooked and perverse generation. Wow, that is powerful!

So why is thankfulness so important? I want you to look at Romans chapter 1, where it is written that many terrible things would happen, and I want you to see what's at the top of the list: "...Although they knew God, they did not glorify Him as God, *nor were thankful, but became futile in their thoughts*, and their foolish hearts were darkened. Professing to be wise, they became fools" (vv. 21,22).

So when you start being unthankful, you open your mind to futile things. That could mean you start worrying about matters that have nothing to do with you. Or you may start having fleshly opinions about people and what they're doing. Their lives have nothing to do with you, yet you have allowed your judgment about their lives to affect your thinking process.

In contrast, thankfulness holds us in a good place both in our thoughts and our emotions. We all need to make sure we maintain a thankful heart.

TEN HEALED LEPERS — ONLY ONE RETURNED TO GIVE THANKS

The example I think of is the story of Jesus and the ten lepers in Luke chapter 17. Jesus was traveling through Samaria and Galilee, and when He entered a certain village, He encountered ten lepers standing at a distance, calling out to Him.

**And they lifted up their voices and said, "Jesus, Master, have
mercy on us!" So when He saw them, He said to them, "Go,
show yourselves to the priests." And so it was that as they
went, they were cleansed.**

Luke 17:13,14

We don't know how long these ten men had been lepers, but
leprosy is a terrible disease that attacks a person's nerves. The
nerves begin to die in a person's extremities so that when one
suffering from leprosy injures himself, he has no feeling and the
wound consequently just gets worse and worse. Leprosy also
attacks the skin, the muscles, and the respiratory system. It is a
horrible disease.

But these ten men had just been cleansed of their leprosy as
they were on their way to the priest! Try to imagine what that was
like for them. They were checking each other out and exclaiming
among themselves, "My arm is clean! I can see out of this eye
again! I can breathe better! Oh, my muscles are working again!"
Imagine the ten men's joy and excitement as they made their way
to the priests, because they were all receiving a miracle!

But then one member of the group did something different
than the rest.

**And one of them, when he saw that he was healed, returned,
and with a loud voice glorified God, and fell down on his
face at His feet, giving Him thanks. And he was a Samaritan.**

Luke 17:15,16

When this man started seeing and feeling this miracle take
place in his body, he said to himself, *I've got to go thank Jesus
for healing me!* The Bible says that this man turned around and
ran back to Jesus and bowed before Him at His feet. The man

may have said something like this: "Oh, Jesus, I don't know what to say — that You have done this for me, a Samaritan. I'm just so thankful! Thank You, Jesus. Truly You are the Messiah, and I glorify You."

What Jesus replied to that man is so significant. He answered this man, "...Were there not ten cleansed? But where are the nine?" (v. 17). *Jesus noticed* that ten received a miracle, but only one came back to give thanks.

We learn something about Jesus here — He notices when we give thanks to Him for what He's done for us. We know this because Jesus is the same yesterday, today, and forever (*see* Hebrews 13:8).

Jesus also notices when we *don't* praise Him. When I read the question that Jesus asked — "I cleansed ten of you. Where are the other nine?" — my first thought was, *Lord, I don't EVER want to be like the nine who didn't return to thank You.*

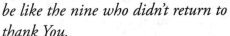

> When I read the question that Jesus asked — "I cleansed ten of you. Where are the other nine?" — my first thought was, *Lord, I don't EVER want to be like the nine who didn't return to thank You.*

For us to be strong in these last days, we have to come to the place, if we're not already walking and living there, where we're a thankful people for all that Jesus has done for us.

Does everything have to be perfect in your life for you to give God wholehearted thanks? No, none of us has a perfect life. I don't have a perfect life. You don't have a perfect life. But the Bible commands all of us to give thanks.

So I encourage you to be thankful for the good things you have received from the Lord. Being thankful is so important, and you can see that Jesus noticed the act of gratitude from the Samaritan who was healed.

THE FRUIT OF THANKFULNESS — *WHOLENESS*

Now, something amazing happened for this Samaritan who returned to give thanks to Jesus. In Luke 17:18 and 19, we read Jesus' response to the man's demonstration of thanksgiving to God:

> **"Were there not any found who returned to give glory to God except this foreigner?" And He said to him, "Arise, go your way. Your faith has made you well."**

That word "well" in the Greek is the word *sozo*, which means *whole* and *healed*. So what was the difference in those nine who didn't come back to thank Jesus and the one who did? The nine were cleansed from the disease, but only one was made completely *whole*.

The one who came back to Jesus was able to fellowship with the Master. In the man's worship and thanksgiving for his healing, some kind of heart exchange took place that drew a response from Jesus to that man.

Think of it — that man had been a leper for years, experiencing all the rejection from society that such a condition would have created. But in that moment of giving thanks, he had placed himself face to face with Jesus.

The man had created an opportunity for Jesus to first cause his body not only to be *healed*, but to be made *whole* from all the ravages of leprosy. That means that even missing parts of his body were restored in that moment! And then beyond the physical healing, Jesus set this man's soul free of all traces of inferiority, rejection, anger, fear — *anything* that held him in mental or emotional bondage. In a moment's time, the man was made whole in every part of his being, and that miracle became possible through the thankfulness of his heart.

When you express thankfulness to Jesus from your heart, you give Him an opportunity not only to heal your body, but also to heal your soul and restore your mind. You see, Jesus came to heal and to save the *whole man*.

Yes, your born-again spirit is as perfect as it's ever going to be. But when it comes to wounds from the past and patterns of wrong thinking, Jesus wants to bring healing to your soul. As you enter into worship for all that He is and into thanksgiving for all His goodness that He has shown you, you open a place of fellowship with Him. In this place, Jesus can by His Spirit touch those places in you that need to be healed and made whole.

> Beyond the physical healing, Jesus set this man's soul free of all traces of inferiority, rejection, anger, fear — *anything* that held him in mental or emotional bondage. In a moment's time, the man was made whole in every part of his being, and that miracle became possible through the thankfulness of his heart.

You may say, "Well, I don't know how to express my thankfulness to God."

The Bible says that praying in tongues is a way to "give thanks well" (*see* 1 Corinthians 14:17). So if you're baptized in the Holy Spirit (*see* Acts 2:4), you can pray in tongues right now from a thankful heart and be assured that you are giving God thanks well.

Or you may say, "But I don't *feel* like giving thanks."

None of this has anything to do with our feelings. When we pray in tongues or read God's Word, we are building ourselves up from the inside out. Proverbs 18:14 (*AMPC*) tells us why this is so important: "The strong spirit of a man sustains him in bodily pain or trouble, but a weak and broken spirit who can raise up or bear?"

So I have a suggestion for you. Every day this next week, read Psalm 103 out loud to the Lord and tell Him *out loud* how thankful you are to Him because He's done so much for you (*see* page 205). You might not feel anything, but that's okay. As you read His Word and start thanking Him from your heart, it will begin to change the way you think. We read earlier about that spiritual principle found in Romans 1:21 — namely, that being thankful helps keep you from thinking about futile things.

None of this has anything to do with our feelings. When we pray in tongues or read God's Word, we are building ourselves up from the inside out.

Honestly, you might not always feel like praising the Lord. But when you do what Jesus asks and continually give thanks to Him, you open a place in your heart to Him where He can work to heal and bring wholeness into your life.

GIVE THANKS TO GOD *IN* EVERYTHING

Certainly it's true that we need Jesus to heal our souls if we ever go through a tragic situation, and I have found that a key to that healing lies in being thankful. I don't believe we're supposed to be thankful *for* tragedy, but we should stay thankful even *in the midst of* tragedy.

First Thessalonians 5:18 says, "In everything give thanks; for this is the will of God in Christ Jesus for you." In how many things are you to give thanks? *In everything*.

That doesn't mean we say, "Oh, Lord, thank You for this cancer. Oh, I thank You that my son is on drugs." No, because those things don't come from God. He doesn't have any evil in Heaven to give, so we're not going to be thanking Him for any evil that presents itself in our lives. But we do thank Him for His goodness and faithfulness even *in the midst of* evil circumstances.

Let me give you an example. Let's say your body is attacked by some kind of illness. You're not to say, "God, I thank You for this illness." But you *are* to recognize Him in the midst of what you're going through. You acknowledge that He is Lord and He is your Healer, and you give Him thanks because He has paid the price for your full salvation and is so worthy of your gratitude and your praise.

No matter what's going on in our lives, every one of us could speak all day long of our thankfulness to Jesus for our salvation!

The Bible says we didn't choose Him, but He chose us (*see* John 15:16). So at any moment of the day, our hearts can turn to Jesus as we say, "Lord, thank You for my salvation that You bought for me through Your precious blood on the Cross. I'm so grateful that I'm going to spend eternity in Heaven with You and not in hell. Thank You that my salvation even includes the healing of my body, mind, and emotions. I'm just so thankful to You, Jesus!"

Praise Strips the Enemy of His Weapons!

Being thankful is so powerful. I want to share a testimony about this regarding my mother. She's been in Heaven now for years, but she was an example while she was on the earth of someone who was always thankful.

When my mother was 85 years old, she was in the hospital for a health issue, and the medical staff gave her some kind of drug that affected her mind for an extended period of time. Mother was acting like she had actually lost her mind, but until that time in the hospital, she had always had a perfect mind. I saw her acting in these strange, abnormal ways and thought, *Lord, this is not Your will. I don't want my mother to lose her mind!*

So I said, "Mama, I'm going to pray for you." Now, I can't tell you that I was operating in great faith when I was praying for my mother; I just prayed a simple prayer for her. But my mother, who was *not* one to lift her hands and worship God, raised her hands straight up and started praising God for her healing!

Over and over, Mama kept saying, "God, you know I am tired, and I don't even want to raise my hands. But I praise You for making me feel better." For 20 minutes with her hands raised, my mother praised the Lord! She just kept praising Him and praising Him and praising Him — and after doing that for 20 minutes, my mother's mind was normal again! As the Bible tells us, where the praises of God's people are, He is right in the midst of them (*see* Psalm 22:3)!

I know Jesus did a miracle for my mother that day. And when she died several years later, her mind was perfect. Jesus touched my mama as she gave thanks to Him in the midst of that trial.

When God's people give thanks, it strips the enemy of his weapons! Remember what happened when Paul and Silas had been beaten and thrown in prison. Acts 16:25 says that at midnight, the two men began to sing praises to God — loud enough for the other prisoners to hear them singing! And *God* also heard their praises and caused an earthquake to break them from their chains (*see* v. 26)!

> When God's people give thanks, it strips the enemy of his weapons!

The jailer saw the open prison doors and prepared to kill himself, thinking the prisoners had all escaped. But Paul and Silas shouted, "Don't harm yourself — we're here!" And not only was the jailer saved, but his whole household got saved (*see* vv. 31-33)!

AVOID THE HARVEST OF A COMPLAINER

As we draw close to the end of this age, I do believe that Jesus wants us to become more thankful than ever before — because if we're not thankful, our minds can start going a different, unproductive direction.

We know that Paul warned us about that direction in Philippians 2:14: "Do all things without complaining and disputing." We live in flesh bodies and tend to want to complain and feel sorry for ourselves. But each day we have a choice: We can go out into our world being thankful to God for His blessings in our lives, or we can go out focused on and complaining about what we *don't* have. Every day of our lives we decide which attitude it will be.

When we make the right choice, verse 15 reveals the outcome: We "…become blameless and harmless, children of God without fault in the midst of a crooked and perverse generation, among whom you shine as lights in the world." So when we're thankful, we shine as lights in the midst of the generation we're born to impact on this earth for God. On the opposite side, if we choose to live as complainers, we can actually cause harm to other people and to ourselves.

A complaining attitude negatively affects our joy and, therefore, our strength. When we complain, we are focusing on what is making us dissatisfied or unhappy, and that opens the door for jealousy of someone else's happiness.

Jealousy is another poisonous emotional state. We can begin to want what another person has,

As we draw close to the end of this age, I do believe that Jesus wants us to become more thankful than ever before — because if we're not thankful, our minds can start going a different, unproductive direction.

which is covetousness, and actually believe we deserve it! When jealousy is allowed to fester, it can ultimately destroy relationships and even our own health (*see* Proverbs 14:30; 27:4; Song of Solomon 8:6).

When we complain, we are focusing on what is making us dissatisfied or unhappy, and that opens the door for jealousy of someone else's happiness.

But there's a way to steer clear of these pitfalls that have the potential to steal our peace, hurt our relationships, and even cause physical issues in our bodies. We have seen that the answer is simple, and our loving Heavenly Father gives it to us in His Word in Philippians 2:14 and First Thessalonians 5:18: "Do *all things* without complaining," and "*in everything* give thanks; for this is the will of God in Christ Jesus for you"!

12

THE POWER OF OUR WORDS

I want to give you one more key to unlocking health and wholeness for your life. This one is possibly the most powerful of all because it is connected to all the rest.

In these last days, knowing how to control your mouth will make all the difference in the world in your walk with God. The devil is working hard to destroy all kinds of relationships by the things people say to each other. To combat that demonic strategy, Christians must be well-equipped by the Word of God to know what to speak in every situation.

Your mouth can either *steal from* or *add to* your own strength. James 3:5 sets the stage with a clear word picture that reveals the power of your words.

In these last days, knowing how to control your mouth will make all the difference in the world in your walk with God.

Even so the tongue is a little member and boasts great things. See how great a forest a little fire kindles!

James 3:5

I know for sure that my tongue has caused a few "forest fires" in my lifetime! That is probably true for you as well. Thank God, we're growing in Him and in the knowledge of His Word! We're turning to Him more and more, and He is developing in us discipline in our hearts and our minds, which is going to help us control our tongue.

In this chapter, I'm going to give you some principles from the Word to help you in this area. You need to know how to avoid starting those fires with your mouth in the first place. And if you do start one, you need to know how to put out that fire before it brings destruction — which most certainly includes a negative impact on your own physical and emotional health.

I want us to look into the book of Proverbs, because it has quite a bit to say on this principle of opening our mouths with wisdom. Solomon, who wrote most of these scriptures (*see* Proverbs 1:1; 10:1; 25:1), was the richest and most powerful king of his time, and in his reign there was no war. I believe we are wise if we listen to the wisdom that Solomon wrote by inspiration of the Holy Spirit in this book.

Let's begin in Proverbs 31, a chapter that describes an amazing and godly woman. This is what is said about the words of her mouth:

She opens her mouth with wisdom, and on her tongue is the law of kindness.

Proverbs 31:26

This is true for males and females alike. I want my mouth to speak according to the law of kindness. I know you do too.

Let's look for a moment at the negative examples God provides on how to avoid the speaking of wrong words from our mouth. For instance, Proverbs 11:22 is a rather interesting scripture:

As a ring of gold in a swine's snout, so is a lovely woman who lacks discretion.

Proverbs 11:22

The woman in this scripture (and, again, this principle applies to men too!) doesn't think of the consequences of her words before she speaks. She just says whatever she wants to say according to whatever way she feels. If she's angry or tired, everyone is going to know it. If she has an opinion, everyone is going to know it.

And this scripture says that the woman is beautiful. Her face is pleasant to look at, yet her mouth says anything she wants to say. She has no discretion or desire to think through what she is about to say. She doesn't take the time to think, *I could really hurt someone's feelings or cause offense if I say that.* Instead of considering the words that would be best to speak, she just says whatever she feels without regard to the possible consequences.

Even if a woman like that is beautiful, the Bible says it's like putting a ring on a pig's nose. In other words, a ring doesn't belong on a pig's nose, and neither does a woman need to have a mouth like the one I just described. The indiscretion of her mouth makes her unattractive, regardless of her physical beauty.

Proverbs 27:15 and 16 give us another vivid illustration of how God views a person with an unrestrained mouth:

A continual dripping on a very rainy day and a contentious woman are alike; whoever restrains her restrains the wind, and grasps oil with his right hand.

The Hebrew word for "dripping" doesn't carry the meaning of just a few drops of water. It's talking about *buckets* of water — water that doesn't just drip, but it pours out and feels as if it will never stop! So if a wife is using her mouth for complaining and fault-finding against her husband, it isn't like drops of water pelting the man. It's more like she is pouring buckets of cold water on him!

I don't know if you've ever seen a woman like that. She might go on and on about how she doesn't like the salary her husband earns. She doesn't like how he talks, how he stands, how he sits, how he treats the children, how he talks to her mother, etc. This type of wife just keeps pouring buckets of criticism on her husband, and her words are such a powerful force that the man cannot escape!

Verse 16 goes on to say, "Whoever restrains her restrains the wind…." This kind of woman is likened to wind — and who can restrain the wind? That's the kind of power this woman wields using the words of her mouth.

The verse continues: "…and grasps oil with his right hand." This woman complains and criticizes so much that it's like she has poured rancid oil on her husband, and he cannot escape the smell or the feel of it.

Although these verses refer specifically to wives, it's important to understand that this principle can be turned around and applied to men as well. A husband's negative words poured out on his wife hold the same destructive force as a wife's negative words poured out on her husband. The power of words knows no gender!

It is truly profound to think of the kind of power we have with our words. God help us use that power for good! May our words always be words that build up and edify (*see* Ephesians 4:29)!

LIFE OR DEATH?
IT'S OUR CHOICE!

The words of our mouth are so very important. Proverbs 18:21 says, "Death and life are in the power of the tongue, and those who love it will eat its fruit." Every day we're choosing which force — death or life — that we're going to release from our mouths through our words.

It's also important that each of us understands that whatever comes out of our mouth is our own responsibility, *not* the responsibility of someone else. We can't blame the wrong things we say on anyone else.

> Whatever comes out of our mouth is our own responsibility, *not* the responsibility of someone else. We can't blame the wrong things we say on anyone else.

"But, Denise, you don't know how they treat me." I understand that you may be facing difficult challenges in your relationships or your circumstances. But if you don't take responsibility for your

own words and you keep trying to blame someone else, you will not be able to make the changes necessary to experience victory in your life. You'll stay the same while you keep blaming others for your situation, and you'll become more and more a victim in your own eyes.

But you're *not* a victim. In Christ Jesus, you are a victor! However, that means you must take responsibility for your words and determine that what comes out of your mouth will bring only good to others.

We want to be carriers only of life, so let's explore just a few of the many things the Word has to say about words that either create death or create life. God has provided great instruction in this area for us to study and obey.

First, Proverbs 18:8 addresses the danger of gossip as one form of "death" that we have to guard against coming out of our mouth.

The words of a talebearer are like tasty trifles, and they go down into the inmost body.

That phrase "tasty trifles" is very telling, reflecting both the attitude of the talebearer and of the one who greedily receives those words into his hearing and his being. It's like the person gossiping is thinking, *Oh, just let me find another morsel to gossip about. It tastes so good — yum, yum!*

This verse goes on to say that before those words of gossip bring their destructive power to the person being gossiped about, they go down into the inmost body of the person speaking or hearing them. That is a direct warning to all who indulge in gossip.

Let's look at one more verse on the subject of gossip. It is amazing what this verse reveals about the destructive power of words that fit in this category!

A man who bears false witness against his neighbor is like a club, a sword, and a sharp arrow.

Proverbs 25:18

That is a powerful verse. It's saying that if we gossip, it's the equivalent of our hurting, maiming, or even killing another person three times in three different ways: once with a club, once with a sword, and once with a sharp arrow. And it's all done with our mouth!

We can't escape this spiritual principle by ignoring it. The Bible says we don't belong to ourselves — we belong to God. And our mouth is part of what belongs to Him.

God isn't mincing words. He is letting us know that in His eyes, when we speak words that hurt people, it is equivalent to hurting, maiming, or even killing them three different ways. That is powerful incentive to commit our tongue to the Lord and ask Him to help us put a watch over our mouth continually!

The Bible says we don't belong to ourselves — we belong to God. And our mouths are part of what belongs to Him.

Proverbs 18:20 gives us further insight into the power of our words:

A man's stomach shall be satisfied from the fruit of his mouth; from the produce of his lips he shall be filled.

In other words, the words we speak provide a supply of either life or death that fills us on the inside. Every day we make the choice regarding the kind of supply that is filling us.

Consider what kind of supply is filling us if we're speaking statements such as the following. All of these statements carry a powerful negative attitude in them.

- "I can't do it."

- "I can't stand it anymore."

- "I'm done. I give up."

- "I don't have anything to give."

- "My life is so pitiful."

When we speak like that, those words of death are not only going into the atmosphere for the enemy to work with, but they are also entering *us* through the gates of our own ears. The Bible says we're actually *filled* with the words we speak — so we need to fill ourselves with words of life that agree with God!

HOLD FAST YOUR CONFESSION OF FAITH!

The principle of keeping our words in agreement with God is key to our living a victorious life in Him. It is essentially what the writer of Hebrews meant when he wrote, "Let us *hold fast the confession* of our hope [expectation] without wavering, for He who promised is faithful" (Hebrews 10:23). To receive from God, we must *keep our words in agreement with God* without wavering.

For instance, let's say that the flu season comes and you start saying, "Well, flu season is here. I'm probably going to get sick." Or perhaps you say, "My husband [or wife] has the flu, so I'm likely going to get the flu, too — and then my children will probably get the flu."

There is a *big* problem with that kind of speech! The words we say carry within them our expectation and faith, so when we use our mouth to say such things, we're exercising our faith in the wrong direction! We're actually saying, "I'm using my faith right now to believe that my children and I will get sick. I expect to get sick!"

Now, I know that's not really what you want, but the principle of God's Word is still true. You might say, "Oh, I'm just speaking the facts. The flu *is* contagious!" But, friend, I encourage you — don't underestimate the effect your words have on the world around you.

The Bible is full of scriptures telling us that our words have authority. Think about this — how did God create the world? He *spoke*. You were made in the image of God and that same power lives in you (*see* Genesis 1:26). How did you get saved? You *confessed* Jesus Christ as your Lord and Savior. Your mouth has so much authority and power; that's why you do *not* want to use your mouth to confess things that actually bring destruction on yourself or others.

What we *do* want to confess is what God has said in His Word about the matter! We must get in agreement with *Him* and speak words of life over our situation: "By the stripes of Jesus, I am healed. I take authority over this virus in the name of Jesus! I hold the blood of

> Your mouth has so much authority and power; that's why you do *not* want to use your mouth to confess things that actually bring destruction on yourself or others.

Jesus over myself and over my family. Lord, I confess before You that You are our Shield!"

You see, *that* is using your mouth to bring God's will on the scene. That is employing the authority of your confession of faith!

THE CONNECTION
BETWEEN *CONFESSION* AND *EXPECTATION*

I want to tell you a short story about confession. Many years ago, Rick and I were living in the U.S., and we were out of God's will. We had started a church that He hadn't told us to start, and we were eating the fruit of doing things our way. We were so poor. We had very little heat in our house, and absolutely no heat in the kitchen — and our refrigerator was empty.

During this difficult and very lean season of our lives, I came across a book entitled, *What You Say Is What You Get* by Don Gossett. So I started reading this book about the power of my words.

I particularly took note of one story that the author related. It was about a man who was having a very hard time financially. He wasn't able to adequately provide for his family, and his refrigerator was empty. So he decided that every time he passed by that refrigerator, he was going to do something different than he had been doing. Instead of saying or thinking, *Oh God, what are we going to do?*, this man decided he would look at his empty refrigerator and shout, "Praise God! Hallelujah!"

So from that moment on, every time the man passed by the refrigerator, he faithfully shouted, "Praise God! Hallelujah!" — and within a week, someone had blessed him and his family with groceries, filling up that refrigerator with food!

Well, as I said, our refrigerator was empty too. So when I read about that man's testimony, I thought, *I'm going to do that!* From that moment on whenever I passed our refrigerator, instead of thinking or saying, "Oh, what are we going to do? Our refrigerator is empty!" — I just started praising the Lord! I'd say, "Hallelujah! Hallelujah!" and just keep on walking!

The Bible says He inhabits the praises of His people (*see* Psalm 22:3). When we give praise and thanksgiving to God, we also give Him the opportunity to work in our lives.

A week after I started using my mouth to praise God and thank Him for His goodness to us, one of our church members called us out of the blue and said, "You know, God has put it on my heart to buy groceries for your family." Then this person went out and bought so many groceries that our refrigerator *and* our cabinets were full!

Why did that happen? Because within my confession of praise for the Lord's provision and His goodness toward us was *expectation* and *faith*!

The Bible says He inhabits the praises of His people. When we give praise and thanksgiving to God, we also give Him the opportunity to work in our lives.

'IT IS WELL!'

I want to give you an Old Testament example of this kind of expectant faith — the faith of the Shunammite woman, whose story is found in Second Kings 4:8-37. Elisha the prophet had prophesied to her that she was going to have a baby in the next year. She and her husband were old, so it would have to be a miracle. But true to the prophet's words, in one year, she held a little baby boy in her arms.

The parents enjoyed that little boy as he grew. But after a few years had passed, the little boy was out with his father in the field when he suddenly became sick. The servant brought the boy to his mother, and this precious little boy died in her lap. But this mother didn't plan a funeral; instead, she began planning a resurrection!

The woman prepared to go to the man of God. Her husband asked, "Where are you going?" She simply said, "It is well" (v. 23). She was confessing, "Everything is good" — even though every-thing *wasn't* good at that moment.

When the woman reached the dwelling of the man of God, his servant came to her. He asked, "Is it well with your son? Is it well with you? Is it well with your husband?"

The woman answered, "It is well."

You see, in this woman's confession was her expectation and her faith — and she didn't give up! She just kept confessing, "It is well."

The simple end to the story is this: The man of God came to this woman's home and raised her son from the dead according to her expectation and confession of faith!

OUR SUPREME EXAMPLE

No example is more powerful than Jesus Christ Himself as Someone who held fast to His confession of faith. Let's look at the confession of Jesus as He stood on trial for His life.

We begin with what Paul wrote about Jesus' good confession in First Timothy 6:13 (*AMPC*):

> **In the presence of God, Who preserves alive all living things, and of Christ Jesus, Who in His testimony before Pontius Pilate made the good confession....**

Then in John 18:34, we see what the apostle Paul was referring to in his letter to Timothy as we read Jesus' response to Pilate's question, "Are You the king of the Jews?"

> **Jesus answered him, "Are you speaking for yourself about this, or did others tell you this concerning Me?"**

That was a very interesting question Jesus posed. Immediately He was speaking to Pilate's heart. Then came Pilate's response:

> **Pilate answered, "Am I a Jew? Your own nation and the chief priests have delivered You to me. What have You done?"**
>
> **John 18:35**

It is so significant how Jesus answered Pilate here. Remember, we just read in First Timothy that Jesus kept His confession before Pontius Pilate. With that in mind, look at how Jesus responded.

> **Jesus answered, "My kingdom is not of this world. If My kingdom were of this world, My servants would fight, so that I should not be delivered to the Jews; but now My kingdom is not from here."**
>
> **Pilate therefore said to Him, "Are You a king then?"**

Jesus answered, "You say rightly that I am a king. For this cause I was born, and for this cause I have come into the world, that I should bear witness to the truth. Everyone who is of the truth hears My voice."

John 18:36,37

Jesus was being treated like a criminal, yet He spoke like a king.

In verse 36, Jesus said the word "kingdom" three times. Then in verse 37, He affirmed that He was indeed a king. He kept His confession before Pontius Pilate. He was being treated like a common criminal, but He carried Himself like a king.

What is the Word of God saying to you here? Even if you are being treated wrongly, and you're being accused or abused by someone's words, you don't have to respond in kind and act like that person is acting or agree with his assessment of you. *You hold fast to who Jesus says that you are!*

- You are the righteousness of God in Christ Jesus (*see* 2 Corinthians 5:21).

- He transferred you out of darkness and placed you into His Kingdom (*see* Colossians 1:13).

- He knew you and planned out your life before the foundation of the world (*see* Ephesians 1:4; 2:10).

- He has washed you clean with His blood (*see* 1 John 1:9).

- He has written your name down in Heaven (*see* Revelation 20:15).

- He has given you the Holy Spirit to dwell within you (*see* Romans 8:9).

- His Spirit is upon you for power (*see* Acts 1:8).

This is your identity. *This* is the confession you hold before the devil, who is the accuser of the brethren. You are just like Jesus, who was treated like a criminal, yet carried Himself like royalty.

How was Jesus able to do that? We see the answer in First Peter 2:23: "Who, when He was reviled, did not revile in return; when He suffered, He did not threaten, but *committed Himself to Him who judges righteously.*"

Jesus was horribly abused by other people speaking to Him grievously. He was insulted; He was demeaned. It wasn't like He had to endure only a little word of abuse here and there. Abuse was *heaped* upon Jesus, yet He refused to revile His abusers in return. He suffered, but He didn't threaten, and First Peter 2:23 says that He kept committing Himself to the Father, the One who judges righteously.

Even if you are being treated wrongly, and you're being accused or abused by someone's words, you don't have to respond in kind and act like that person is acting or agree with his assessment of you. *You hold fast to who Jesus says that you are!*

It's the same for you and me when the enemy's pressure keeps piling on, whether through other people's critical words, through painful physical symptoms, through doubts that bombard our mind, etc. We just have to keep committing ourselves to our Father, the One who judges righteously.

That's what Jesus did. He kept committing Himself to the Father again and again. Jesus never reviled; He never threatened. He never returned the abuse He was receiving. He simply stayed in the will of the Father and refused to budge in His heart and mind — *or His mouth* — from what God had said to Him.

What can we say about this when it comes to the words of *our* mouth? Jesus is our Example. The same power that raised Him from the dead lives within us by His Spirit (*see* Romans 6:10,11; 8:11). We can never say, "I can't help the words of my mouth. It's their fault my words are negative." No, the Word of God is planted in our heart; the Holy Ghost dwells within us. And if we submit our tongue to Him, He is going to help us hold fast to our confession of faith!

HEALTH TO ALL OUR FLESH

Proverbs 4:20-22 provides the divine instruction we need to keep our mouth speaking only words of life.

My son, give attention to my words; incline your ear to my sayings. Do not let them depart from your eyes; keep them in the midst of your heart; for they are life to those who find them, and health to all their flesh.

Remember, the Holy Spirit is the One who wrote this instruction. He knows exactly what you need to do and say to walk in healing and health.

I suggest you make a commitment before the Lord to read the Bible at least 30 minutes a day. I promise you, staying faithful to that one commitment will change your life. As you obey the Holy Spirit's instruction and immerse yourself in God's Word, you will begin to experience the life of God by the power of the Spirit that is contained in His words.

And this is what He promises — that His words are *life* to those who find them and *health* to all their flesh. That promise is true for *you*.

I want to share with you a testimony along this line that I heard many years ago when Rick and I were on vacation. We were eating dinner at a restaurant and talking with the waitress who was serving us. She told us about the hard work that her job required, serving tables both day and night. I started sharing with her about Jesus, and she replied, "Actually, I'm a Christian. I'm working in this place so I can make money to send home to my family."

As you obey the Holy Spirit's instruction and immerse yourself in God's Word, you will begin to experience the life of God by the power of the Spirit that is contained in His words.

Then this waitress began to share her amazing testimony. "When I first took this job," she said, "I had stage-four pancreatic cancer in my body. But I took to heart what God says in Proverbs 4 — that His Word is health to all my flesh."

The woman related how she began to make a practice of reading through the Bible. Every night when she got in at midnight from work, she would open her Bible and read, no matter how tired she felt. By the end of two months, she had read the entire Bible — and then she found out there was absolutely no more cancer in her body!

Why? Because when God's words are kept and treasured in the midst of your heart, the life in those words will produce life in you and health to all your flesh!

Think about that phrase "*all* your flesh." That includes your eyes, your ears, your heart, your lungs, your pancreas, your liver, your intestines, your kidneys, your skin, your legs, your feet, your mind and emotions, etc. — it simply includes *all* your flesh!

As you read the Word of God, listen to the Word of God, and confess with your mouth the Word of God, you are planting those words deep into your heart. And as you make a determined practice of doing this, day after day after day, the life that resides in God's Word becomes life to *you* and healing to all your flesh.

Friend, what a powerful exhortation from God's Word! He is telling us, "You don't have to be sick! Read the Word. Put it in your eyes; listen to it with your ears; keep it in your heart. As you do, it's going to bring life to you!"

PUT A GUARD ON YOUR MOUTH

Finally, I want to give you a few key scriptures regarding the good that our tongue can do when we speak words of life.

Proverbs 12:18 provides the contrast. It starts out with the effect of negative words when we use our tongue for evil: "There is one who speaks like the piercings of a sword...." Our words have the ability to pierce someone's soul. But then look at the rest of the verse: "...But the tongue of the wise promotes health."

Your words, when they come from your heart by the wisdom of God, are containers of life that bring health and healing to those who hear them. Your words of life carry God's healing power to your own body as well. Proverbs 16:24 confirms this: "Pleasant words are like a honeycomb, sweetness to the soul and health to the bones."

It's our choice what kind of words we speak. We can choose every day to renew our mind with the Word and depend on the Holy Spirit's help to keep a guard over our mouth. As we do, Proverbs 21:23 tells us that we keep ourselves protected from the enemy's strategies against us: "Whoever guards his mouth and tongue keeps his soul from troubles."

In these last days, you can learn how to use your tongue only for good. I believe you want to stay strong and experience wholeness in every area of your life. And I believe you desire to help and strengthen others through your words.

Your words, when they come from your heart by the wisdom of God, are containers of life that bring health and healing to those who hear them.

So make David's prayer in Psalm 141:3 your daily prayer: "Set a guard, O Lord, over my mouth; keep watch over the door of my lips." And I encourage you to pray this prayer of commitment:

Father God, right now as I look to You, I commit myself to using my tongue only to speak words that are for others' good and for Your glory. I repent right now for the times I have spoken words that brought death into a situation. Please cleanse me with Your blood and put a guard over my mouth that allows only words of life to come through. I confess that Your Word lives strong in me, and I give You all the glory. In Jesus' name. Amen.

13

~

GOD HAS A MIRACLE FOR *YOU*!

So much has been said in the previous chapters to help you *know that you know* that Jesus is your Healer and that He has a miracle just for you. And that is the bottom line, my friend. Since Jesus was a Miracle Worker 2,000 years ago, He is a Miracle Worker today. He is not just the One you read about in the Bible who healed people. Jesus is *your* Miracle Worker, because He is the same yesterday, today, and forever (*see* Hebrews 13:8)!

A miracle is something that happens instantly. In one moment, the natural circumstances are what they are — but then something supernatural happens, and everything is completely different in the next moment.

God performed many miracles in the Old Testament, but I'll just mention one here — the parting of the Red Sea. The children of Israel were facing imminent death. Pharaoh's army was right behind them, ready to overtake them, and right in front of them was the Red Sea.

No sea naturally parts to provide a path to cross over to the other side. But as Moses stood there holding up his rod, that sea parted through God's miracle-working power! The Israelites were staring death in the face, but after God intervened, they stood and watched as the enemy army was drowned by the very sea that had parted to save them (*see* Exodus 14)!

A Quick Review — Jesus' Miracle-Working Power

We've already discussed several miracles in the ministry of Jesus — the woman with the issue of blood, Jairus' daughter, blind Bartimaeus, etc. Miracles truly abounded throughout Jesus' earthly ministry.

We talked about the day Jesus had just come down from the mountain, and a leper came and worshiped at Jesus' feet, saying, "Lord, if You're willing, make me clean" (*see* Matthew 8:1-3). Jesus stretched out His hand and touched the leper, and He said, "I am willing. Be clean." And the next word is "immediately" — because *immediately* that man was cleansed of leprosy. He experienced a miracle!

We discussed how horrible leprosy is. The leper was rejected by society. He could lose parts of his body and even his ability to breathe. Sometimes leprosy could make the person blind. That's how this man was living — but in one second, the miracle-working power of God touched that man, and he was completely healed!

We talked about the story of the woman with the issue of blood who had been bleeding for 12 years (*see* Mark 5:25-34).

In Jewish society at that time, a woman was rejected if she suffered from that condition. Anyone she touched would be made unclean. If someone even sat down in a place where she'd sat, that person would be unclean. And this had been going on in this woman's life for *12 years*. This woman had been going from doctor to doctor to doctor, but she hadn't found anyone who could help her.

Then the woman heard about Jesus and began to make her way to Him. She said to herself, *If I can just touch the hem of His garment, I'll be healed.* She finally reached Jesus through the crowd and touched the hem of His garment. And the Bible says that Jesus immediately knew power went out of Him — and *immediately* the flow of blood from the woman stopped.

Jesus brings His miracles with Him wherever He goes!

You can see all around us how sickness and disease steal from our lives. But Jesus' miracle-working, healing power reverses sickness and disease and gives us our lives back! Oh, what a wonderful Savior!

We looked at the story of Jairus, a very powerful man in the synagogue (*see* Mark 5:22-24, 35-42). Jairus heard that his daughter had died soon after he had reached Jesus to ask Him to heal her. But with the words, "…Do not be afraid; only believe," Jesus got Jairus' focus back on faith for a miracle (*see* Mark 5:36).

Jesus' miracle-working, healing power reverses sickness and disease and gives us our lives back! Oh, what a wonderful Savior!

Jesus went with Jairus to where the body of his daughter lay. And when Jesus took the child by the hand and said, "Little girl, I say to you, arise" — immediately the girl rose up and started walking around!

That father could have lived the rest of his life without his little girl — but the love of Jesus and the miracle-working power of God came into that house and raised his little daughter from the dead!

AND A FEW MORE OF JESUS' MIRACLES!

We also talked about the healing of blind Bartimaeus, and in Matthew chapter 20, we see the healing of two other blind men. It says in verse 30 that the two blind men were sitting by the road, and they could hear people passing by. Somehow these two men knew that Jesus was passing by, and they began to cry out: "Have mercy on us, O Lord, Son of David!" Just as in the case of Bartimaeus, the people in the crowd told the blind men to be quiet, but the two just kept screaming louder: "Have mercy on us, O Lord, Son of David!" (v. 31).

Then Jesus stood still and called the two blind men to come. He asked them, "What do you want Me to do for you?" (v. 32).

"Lord, that our eyes may be opened!" the two men answered (v. 33).

Verse 34 says that Jesus had compassion, and He touched their eyes. And immediately their eyes were opened!

Think of these two blind men. All their lives, they hadn't been able to see their own hands; they had never seen their parents; they couldn't see a tree or the sun, moon, or sky. But in one split second, everything about their lives changed! One moment they couldn't see anything, and the next moment they could see everything perfectly!

In Mark 7, we see Jesus perform another healing miracle. The people brought to Jesus a deaf man with a speech impediment (*see* v. 32). They wanted Jesus to lay His hands on this man to heal him, but Jesus did something different instead:

> **And He took him aside from the multitude, and put His fingers in his ears, and He spat and touched his tongue. Then, looking up to heaven, He sighed, and said to him, "Ephphatha," that is, "Be opened." Immediately his ears were opened, and the impediment of his tongue was loosed, and he spoke plainly.**
>
> **Mark 7:33-35**

Now, we don't know why Jesus spat — but we know that He hates deafness. He hates *any* spirit or disease or malady that would take a person's hearing or speech. We also know that Jesus did only what He saw His Father do (*see* John 5:19). And we know that Jesus' method in this situation was effective! Verse 35 says that immediately the man's ears were opened and he spoke plainly! *That* is the miracle-working power of God!

TESTIMONIES
OF THE MIRACLE-WORKING POWER OF GOD

I remember one doctor saying to me, "If you leave that physical issue alone and you don't do anything about it, it will just get worse." That is the course of nature, but a miracle is the power of God *interrupting* the course of nature!

My own husband Rick experienced a great miracle that interrupted the course of nature when he was just a young teenager and new to the things of the Spirit. Rick was born with his kidneys conjoined (sometimes called "horseshoe kidneys") and situated on only one side of his body. This was beginning to cause young Rick physical problems. But then he went to a church meeting where the Word of God was being preached and the power of God was moving — and everything changed in a moment!

A miracle is the power of God *interrupting* the course of nature!

During the meeting, Rick answered the minister's invitation to come forward and have hands laid on him. Rick didn't say anything to the minister, but God knew his condition. The minister simply touched him, and immediately the power of God went through his kidneys and recreated them. In an instant, Rick's kidneys became completely normal! From that moment to this, Rick has had two healthy kidneys positioned normally on each side of his body. It was truly a miracle!

I've told you my testimony about my face. For 13 years I suffered with that skin disease, going from doctor to doctor, being rejected by my peers, being made fun of, and suffering continual pain and embarrassment. But one night I went to bed just as I had for 13 years, and when I woke up the next morning, a miracle had happened in the night and my face was completely healed. That is the miracle-working power of God!

I remember one woman in our church who suffered an injury at birth, and she couldn't stand up straight. Then came a word of knowledge during a meeting about God straightening out someone's legs. In that moment, the Spirit of God touched that woman's hip, and immediately she was healed! Her life had been one way for 30 years. But in one moment, her life changed to another way as she stood straight and tall and *healed*, praising the Lord!

I'm also remembering a friend who was really suffering from COVID. The medical staff was about to put him on a ventilator, and he was waiting in his hospital room. Suddenly a cool breeze came into that room, and the power of God touched that man. He went home from the hospital the next day — miraculously healed!

IT's TIME FOR *YOUR* MIRACLE!

Again, I want to stress to you that Jesus is the same yesterday, today, and forever. And His power is extended to *you* right now.

Jesus walked the earth as the express image of the Father. Everything we see Jesus doing in the gospels was an expression of the Father's heart.

Then through Jesus' beating, crucifixion, and death, He continued to express the will of the Father. Jesus carried blindness on the Cross. He carried cancer on the Cross. He carried heart problems on the Cross. He carried skin problems on the Cross. He carried every disease known to man on the Cross so that He could bring your miracle to you! That is His will right now as you read these words.

What is it that you need from God? Do you need His healing power to touch your body? His power is right there with you right

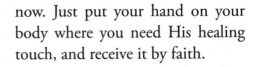

> Oh, I urge you to reach out to Jesus and receive His power for your healing right now! Believe Him for *whatever* you need! Healing, peace, freedom — all of this is Jesus' heart for you.

now. Just put your hand on your body where you need His healing touch, and receive it by faith.

Oh, I urge you to reach out to Jesus and receive His power for your healing right now! Believe Him for *whatever* you need! Healing, peace, freedom — all of this is Jesus' heart for you. That is His love for you. As He suffered on the Cross, He *took upon Himself* whatever condition, sickness, or struggle you are dealing with.

You can know beyond a shadow of a doubt that Jesus not only *can* heal you, but He absolutely *wants* to heal you. He is a miracle-working God, and He has a miracle for *you*!

PRAYER FOR HEALING

In Hebrews 4:16, the Holy Spirit invites you to come boldly before the throne of grace that you might receive the help you need.

If there is sickness or pain in your body, place your hand on that part of your body. Right now I'm agreeing with you. We're touching the hem of Jesus' garment together. We receive His healing power on your behalf in Jesus' name.

Jesus' presence is right there with you by His Spirit as you conclude your reading of this book. So whatever you couldn't do before, I encourage you to begin doing it by faith in Jesus' name!

If you couldn't see very well out of one or both of your eyes, start reading something. If you couldn't move a certain part of your body, start moving it right now. If you couldn't move your arm, try to move your arm. If you couldn't move your fingers, try to move your fingers. If you couldn't walk, start walking!

Jesus is the Healer, and He is alive. He is the same yesterday, today, and forever. It's by your faith in who He is that He is touching you right now. So receive in Jesus' mighty name!

If you have had any kind of physical healing touch as you read this book, please write or email us and let us know (*see* page 208 for contact information).

Remember, there is power in your testimony, so tell someone about His healing power! He's not just the Healer of the Bible — He's *your* Healer today!

PRAYER FOR SALVATION

When Jesus Christ comes into your life, you are immediately emancipated — totally set free from the bondage of sin! If you have never received Jesus as your personal Savior, it is time to experience this new life for yourself. The first step to freedom is simple. Just pray this prayer from your heart:

Lord, I can never adequately thank You for all You did for me on the Cross. I am so undeserving, Jesus, but You came and gave Your life for me anyway. I repent for rejecting You, and I turn away from my life of rebellion and sin right now. I turn to You and receive You as my Savior, and I ask You to wash away my sin and make me completely new in You by Your precious blood. I thank You from the depths of my heart for doing what no one else could do for me. Had it not been for Your willingness to lay down Your life for me, I would be eternally lost.

Thank You, Jesus, that I am now redeemed by Your blood. On the Cross, You bore my sin, my sickness, my pain, my lack of peace, and my suffering. Your blood has removed my sin, washed me whiter than snow, and given me rightstanding with the Father. I have no need to be ashamed of my past sins because I am now a new creature in You. Old things have passed away, and all things have become new because I am in Jesus Christ (see 2 Corinthians 5:17).

Because of You, Jesus, today I am forgiven; I am filled with peace; and I am a joint-heir with You! Satan no longer has a right to lay any claim on me. From a grateful heart, I will faithfully serve You the rest of my days!

If you prayed this prayer from your heart, something amazing has happened to you. No longer a servant to sin, you are now a servant of Almighty God. The evil spirits that once required your all-inclusive servitude no longer possess the authority to control you or dictate your destiny!

As a result of your decision to turn your life over to Jesus Christ, your eternal home has been decided forever. Heaven will now be your permanent address for all eternity. God's Spirit has moved into your human spirit, and you have become the "temple of God" (*see* 1 Corinthians 6:19). What a miracle! To think that God, by His Spirit, now lives inside you!

Now you have a new Lord and Master, and His name is Jesus. From this moment on, the Spirit of God will work in you and supernaturally energize you to fulfill God's will for your life. Everything will change for you as you yield to His leadership — and it's all going to change for the best!

BE AN INSTRUMENT OF GOD'S HEALING POWER

Remember, Jesus released the power of God to others everywhere He went — and the power of God is in *you*. You have Jesus' word for it! In Mark 16:17 and 18, He said, "...These signs will follow those who believe: In My name...they will lay hands on the sick, and they will recover."

So when you sense His compassion rising up in you and you so desire to see someone be healed, just say, "Lord, I realize this is Your desire to heal that I'm sensing, so I'm just going to release my faith in Your power that's in me as I lay hands on this person."

It's truly the power of God within you that makes all the difference. Your hands are simply a vehicle of transfer for that healing power to be released from you into another person.

Keep learning about the power of God in you. As you pray in other tongues, become more and more aware of His power in you, and keep stretching your hands forth to bless humanity.

Don't let the devil stop you with his discouragement! Just decide that you're going to continue to obey God in this matter, no matter what. Whatever good God wants you to do in laying hands on the sick, you're going to do.

I can promise you the devil is against it. He hates God, and he hates you because you're made in the image of God. And he is against the power of God in you. When you pray by faith in the name of Jesus, God's power is released through you. So if the devil tries to discourage you, just say, "Okay, Mr. Devil, I'm going to lay my hands on even more people to see them healed! I recognize the power of God in me, but it's not about me; it's about my God *in* me!"

Many others before you — some who even had healing ministries — have experienced similar challenges of discouragement. I heard one minister say, "It seems that every time I pray for someone, they get sicker!" But he didn't stop, and to this day, God uses that man in a powerful way to bring healing to many.

So don't you stop being an instrument of God's healing, delivering power. You have the Spirit of God inside you, and you're a believer. And as you keep praying for the sick, you *will* begin to see them recover!

PSALM 103

As an act of thanksgiving, read this psalm out loud to the Lord. When you are finished, take a moment to thank Him for all He has done for you.

Bless the Lord, O my soul;
And all that is within me, bless His holy name!
Bless the Lord, O my soul,
And forget not all His benefits:
Who forgives all your iniquities,
Who heals all your diseases,
Who redeems your life from destruction,
Who crowns you with lovingkindness and tender mercies,
Who satisfies your mouth with good things,
So that your youth is renewed like the eagle's.

The Lord executes righteousness
And justice for all who are oppressed.
He made known His ways to Moses,
His acts to the children of Israel.
The Lord is merciful and gracious,
Slow to anger, and abounding in mercy.
He will not always strive with us,
Nor will He keep His anger forever.
He has not dealt with us according to our sins,
Nor punished us according to our iniquities.

For as the heavens are high above the earth,
So great is His mercy toward those who fear Him;
As far as the east is from the west,
So far has He removed our transgressions from us.
As a father pities his children,
So the Lord pities those who fear Him.

For He knows our frame;
He remembers that we are dust.

As for man, his days are like grass;
As a flower of the field, so he flourishes.
For the wind passes over it, and it is gone,
And its place remembers it no more.
But the mercy of the Lord is from everlasting
to everlasting
On those who fear Him,
And His righteousness to children's children,
To such as keep His covenant,
And to those who remember His commandments
to do them.

The Lord has established His throne in heaven,
And His kingdom rules over all.

Bless the Lord, you His angels,
Who excel in strength, who do His word,
Heeding the voice of His word.
Bless the Lord, all you His hosts,
You ministers of His, who do His pleasure.
Bless the Lord, all His works,
In all places of His dominion.

Bless the Lord, O my soul!

ABOUT THE AUTHOR

Denise Renner is an able minister, a mentor to women, an author, and a classically trained vocalist. Alongside her husband Rick Renner, Denise spent years ministering in the U.S. before moving in 1991 with their family to the former Soviet Union, where they began their international ministry. Since that time, Rick and Denise have proclaimed the Gospel throughout the vast region of the former USSR. Their ministry reaches a potential audience of millions in both hemispheres of the world via television, satellite, and the Internet.

Rick and Denise reside in Moscow. Together they founded the Moscow Good News Church, which today they help lead along with their son and daughter-in-law Paul and Polina Renner. Denise directs a large women's ministry in the church that affects women from all over Moscow. Thousands of women have been mentored and trained in her marriage seminars in person or online. Meanwhile, whether in historic concert halls, local churches, or her ministry to women, Denise still regularly ministers in music, using her remarkably gifted voice to bring Christ's burden-destroying anointing to those in need of His touch.

CONTACT RENNER MINISTRIES

For further information
about RENNER Ministries,
please contact the office nearest you,
or visit the ministry website at:
www.renner.org

ALL USA CORRESPONDENCE:
RENNER Ministries
1814 W. Tacoma St.
Broken Arrow, OK 74012
(918) 496-3213
Or 1-800-RICK-593
Email: renner@renner.org
Website: www.renner.org

MOSCOW OFFICE:
RENNER Ministries
P. O. Box 789
101000, Moscow, Russia
+7 (495) 727-1467
Email: blagayavestonline@ignc.org
Website: www.ignc.org

RIGA OFFICE:
RENNER Ministries
Unijas 99
Riga LV-1084, Latvia
+371 67802150
Email: church@goodnews.lv
Website: www.goodnews.lv

OXFORD OFFICE:
RENNER Ministries
Box 7, 266 Banbury Road
Oxford OX2 7DL, United Kingdom
+44 1865 521024
Email: europe@renner.org

WITH US!

facebook.com/rickrenner • facebook.com/rennerdenise
youtube.com/rennerministries • youtube.com/deniserenner
instagram.com/rickrrenner • instagram.com/rennerministries_
instagram.com/rennerdenise

BOOKS BY DENISE RENNER

Do You Know What Time It Is?*

The Gift of Forgiveness*

Jesus Is Your Healer*

Redeemed From Shame*

Unstoppable*

Who Stole Cinderella?*

*Digital version available for Kindle, Nook, and iBook, and other eBook formats.

Note: Books by Denise Renner
are available for purchase at:
www.renner.org

BOOKS BY RICK RENNER

Apostles and Prophets
Build Your Foundation*
Chosen by God*
Christmas — The Rest of the Story
Dream Thieves*
Dressed To Kill*
The Holy Spirit and You*
How To Keep Your Head on Straight in a World Gone Crazy*
How To Receive Answers From Heaven!*
Igniting a Powerful Prayer Life
Insights on Successful Leadership*
Last-Days Survival Guide*
A Life Ablaze*
Life in the Combat Zone*
A Light in Darkness, Volume One,
   Seven Messages to the Seven Churches series
The Love Test*
My Peace-Filled Day
My Spirit-Empowered Day
No Room for Compromise, Volume Two,
   Seven Messages to the Seven Churches series
Paid in Full*
The Point of No Return*
Repentance*
Signs You'll See Just Before Jesus Comes*
Sparkling Gems From the Greek Daily Devotional 1*
Sparkling Gems From the Greek Daily Devotional 2*
Spiritual Weapons To Defeat the Enemy*
Ten Guidelines To Help You Achieve Your Long-Awaited Promotion!*
Testing the Supernatural
365 Days of Increase
365 Days of Power
Turn Your God-Given Dreams Into Reality*
Unlikely — Our Faith-Filled Journey to the Ends of the Earth*
Why We Need the Gifts of the Holy Spirit*
The Will of God — The Key to Your Success*
You Can Get Over It*

*Digital version available for Kindle, Nook, and iBook.
Note: Books by Rick Renner are available for purchase at:
www.renner.org

UNSTOPPABLE

Pressing Through Fear, Offense, and Negative Opinions To Fulfill God's Purpose

By Denise Renner

208 pages
(Paperback)

God has given every one of us a unique supply of His Spirit — with individual gifts and callings — that we are to contribute to the Body of Christ and to the plans and purposes of God on earth.

But what stops so many from entering this place of blessing and falling short of fulfilling their God-given destiny? The obstacles are plenteous because the enemy is most threatened when a believer takes his or her place in the perfect will of God. Some of these hindrances include fear, offense, and the negative opinions of others. But the good news is, God has given us power through His Word and His Spirit to overcome every obstacle and to *gloriously* manifest our supply for the blessing and benefit of others.

In her book *Unstoppable*, Denise Renner brings fresh insight from God's Word on how we can overcome key hindrances — whether it's fear of man, rejection, unforgiveness, other people's negative opinions, or even our own poor opinion of ourselves — that the enemy exploits to try to prevent our God-given gifts and talents from being used to bless others.

No one else can take your place; your part is absolutely crucial to God's plan. So don't let anyone or anything stop you from doing what Jesus wants you to do or from receiving what He wants you to receive. This book will help you be *unstoppable* as you push past every obstacle you are facing and keep pressing toward the glorious prize that awaits you in Christ Jesus!

To order, visit us online at: **www.renner.org**

Book Resellers: Contact Harrison House at 800-722-6774
or visit **www.HarrisonHouse.com** for quantity discounts.

WHO STOLE CINDERELLA?

192 pages
(Paperback)

In **Who Stole Cinderella?**, Denise Renner shows why "happily ever after" is not a gift for a selected few, but rather an art that anyone can master who is willing to learn. With genuine warmth and candor, Denise recounts the journey of her own struggles in marriage and the unique insights she learned along the way to attaining emotional health and happiness. Your life will be enriched by the biblical wisdom Denise imparts and the originality with which she sheds light on your path to *happily ever after* and shows you right where to begin again if you've lost your way.

Even if the clock shows "past midnight" in your marriage, don't give up on your dream of experiencing a happy ending. Cinderella and Prince Charming are not lost — they just need to be rediscovered *God's way*!

"This teaching, like precious pearls, has been obtained by diving into the deep to learn of God and His ways over the course of many years. It is yours for the reading — but believe me when I tell you that it has cost Denise extravagantly."

— Rick Renner

To order, visit us online at: **www.renner.org**

Book Resellers: Contact Harrison House at 800-722-6774 or visit **www.HarrisonHouse.com** for quantity discounts.

Do You Know What Time It Is?

You may have lost some opportunities in the past because you kept putting off what God told you to do. But it's never too late to stop wasting time! Denise Renner states: "These are crucial times we live in, and how we spend our time is a very serious matter. We must take the opportunities we have available right now to do what God has called us to do, because the clock is ticking, and time is passing us by." Let Denise inspire you to get back on track with God's purposes for your life as you pursue all that He has for you — every minute of every day!

The Gift of Forgiveness

The act of forgiveness is one of the greatest yet most difficult commands that Jesus asks of us. Denise Renner draws both from the Word and from her own life experience to guide the reader from the depths of pain and despair to the ultimate act of love and emotional freedom through the act of forgiving others.

Redeemed From Shame

In this book, Denise Renner demonstrates how the love of Jesus through the power of the Holy Spirit can set anyone free who has been emotionally crippled by shame in his or her life. Let the redeemed of the Lord say, "I am whole!" The message of *Redeemed From Shame* will change your life!

*Digital version available for Kindle, Nook, iBook, and other eBook formats. For retail purchases and more information, visit us online at: **www.renner.org**.

IGNITING A POWERFUL PRAYER LIFE

A Sparkling Gems From the Greek
Guided Devotional Journal

256 pages
(Paperback)

Igniting a Powerful Prayer Life: A Sparkling Gems From the Greek Guided Devotional Journal can take you from feeling overwhelmed by the signs of the times to enjoying a serene sense of wholeness and well-being as you walk and live in God's presence.

You are not impotent against the struggles of broken families and relationships, decaying morality, rumors of wars, and unstable economies! The Father longs for you to release His power in your sphere through prayer. You only need to know how.

In *Igniting a Powerful Prayer Life*, Rick Renner uses scriptural principles and spiritual wisdom that can set ablaze in your heart a passion for potent prayer. Each lesson in this 31-day journal also includes a prayer and a confession to put the Word in your mouth and stimulate a fervent, effectual prayer life.

Topics and word studies include:

- Unleashing new prayer dimensions.

- Praying with boldness and confidence.

- Moving from fear to faith and from defeat to victory.

- Experiencing Jesus as our personal Intercessor.

Don't stand by and let the enemy oppress or destroy you *or* your family. Use this guided journal to ignite your prayer life and set your world *on fire* with the power of God!

To order, visit us online at: **www.renner.org**

Book Resellers: Contact Harrison House at 800-722-6774 or visit **www.HarrisonHouse.com** for quantity discounts.

MY SPIRIT-EMPOWERED DAY
A SPARKLING GEMS FROM THE GREEK
GUIDED DEVOTIONAL JOURNAL

240 pages
(Paperback)

When faced with life's difficulties, do you long for a personal coach to guide you? Do you feel inadequate, even powerless, to achieve what God has asked you to do?

You can experience the same inseparable union with the Holy Spirit that empowered Jesus during His earthly ministry! With the Holy Spirit's help, *you* can participate for yourself with His mission to be your ultimate Comforter, Advocate, Counselor, and Friend.

In *My Spirit-Empowered Day: A Sparkling Gems From the Greek Guided Devotional Journal*, Rick Renner shows you how to escape a powerless Christian life. This interactive journal includes thought-provoking questions that will engage your heart and mind to go deeper with the Holy Spirit.

Through 31 insightful devotional entries, Rick unveils from the Greek text the purpose of the Holy Spirit in a Christian's life. Rick's teaching will help you understand the workings of the Holy Spirit, discover how to receive divine guidance, and exercise spiritual power and authority.

Experience a life of close fellowship with the Holy Spirit and see your life flourish under His favor!

To order, visit us online at: **www.renner.org**

Book resellers: Contact Harrison House at 800-722-6774 or visit **www.HarrisonHouse.com** for quantity discounts.

PAID IN FULL
AN IN-DEPTH LOOK AT THE DEFINING MOMENTS
OF CHRIST'S PASSION

320 pages
(Paperback)

In *Paid in Full: An In-Depth Look at the Defining Moments of Christ's Passion*, Rick Renner offers unforgettable insights into the heart, emotions, and humanity of Jesus in His final days on the earth. Providing a brilliant historical backdrop from his studies of New Testament Greek, Rick guides you on an uncommon journey through each of Christ's encounters along His way from Gethsemane to Golgotha.

Jesus' responses to betrayal and suffering reveal rich, practical applications for our own lives when we're faced with disappointment and pain. As you gain a more intimate glimpse into Jesus' final hours and the great love He displayed, you will be moved in a way you will never forget and will gain more confidence than ever that God's plan for your life will stand!

Your redemption had a price. Discover just how completely that price was *paid in full*!

To order, visit us online at: **www.renner.org**

Book Resellers: Contact Harrison House at 800-722-6774 or visit **www.HarrisonHouse.com** for quantity discounts.

Personal Notes

_____

_____

_____

_____

_____

_____

_____

_____

_____

_____

_____

_____

_____

_____

_____

_____

_____

_____

_____

_____

Personal Notes

Personal Notes

Personal Notes

Personal Notes

Personal Notes

Equipping Believers to Walk in the Abundant Life
John 10:10b

Connect with us for fresh content and news about forthcoming books from your favorite authors...

Facebook @ HarrisonHousePublishers

Instagram @ HarrisonHousePublishing

www.harrisonhouse.com